BASKETBALL MY TEACHER
JESUS MY SAVIOR

BY BRANDON "BREEZE" DAWSON

Copyright © 2022 by Brandon "Breeze" Dawson

Love. Faith. Endurance. LLC supports copyright. Copyright encourages creativity, gives a voice to the voiceless, and allows artists to be exactly who they are. Thank you for purchasing an approved version of this book and acting in accordance with copyright laws by not reproducing or transmitting in any form or by any means electronic, mechanical, photocopying, recording, or otherwise without prior written permission from Brandon "Breeze" Dawson and Love. Faith. Endurance. LLC.

All scripture references are taken from the New Living Translation (NLT), King James Version (KJV), New King James Version (NKJV), New International Version (NIV), and the English Standard Version (ESV).

Acknowledgements

In many autobiographies I've seen the acknowledgements page in the back of the book, but I'd like to give my thanks on the front end. There are so many people that have been a part of my life who've played a role in creating this book and aren't even aware of it. People like my family, friends, mentors, coaches, teammates, and teachers. But on this page, I'd like to thank those who have had a hand in creating the physical document that you hold before you. The first person I'd like to thank is my wife, Nikki, who took the back cover photo, has been a sounding board, and supported me in every way during this project. I couldn't have done this without you, Lady.

Next, I would like to thank the amazing people at Studio Nine, Giulia "Soleil" Cleveland and Stephan "Apollo" Fields for working so diligently with me throughout this process. Giulia shot the promotional video and Stephan took the front cover photo. Without them, this project wouldn't be what it is.

Lastly, I would like to thank Chelcey Farrar who used her talents to create the cover. Her eye for design and perseverance was essential in creating a product so appealing.

Each of these individuals helped me bring a longtime vision of mine to life and for that I'm extremely thankful.

Dedication

For a long time, I've known that the things I've gone through wouldn't be in vain. My hope has always been that my story could inspire others so they wouldn't make the same mistakes that I've made, and so they wouldn't waste time like I've wasted it. With that being said, I dedicate this book to Jesus, the one who used the trials that I've gone through to strengthen me. He also helped me realize that the things that I've gone through weren't just for me; these trials were to help those coming behind me navigate the treacherous terrain. I also dedicate this book to those who have a dream or a vision and aren't able to see how it will come to pass. I encourage you to trust God with this dream or vision; He's the one that gave it to you, and He's the one that can lead you to it.

Message to the Reader

Dear Reader,

Thank you for supporting me and taking the time to read this book. Your support means so much to me and I hope that you're blessed by these words. The journey you're about to embark on through these pages is my testimony. The Bible says that we "overcome by the blood of the lamb, and the word of our testimony" (Revelation 12:11), so this is me overcoming all the things that have slowed me down and so easily tripped me up in my past. My hope is that as you read about the trials that I've gone through, you're inspired to trust God as you go through yours as well. Then, after you've made it through your trials, your testimony will inspire someone else to get through theirs.

And as you overcome, remember to do it with Love, Faith, and Endurance.

Brandon "Breeze" Dawson

Table of Contents

Desire	12
Role Play	16
Hope	20
Fear	24
Respect	30
Leaders	38
40 Pills	46
Against the Grain	54
Focus	58
Eagle's Wings	66
Vision	74
Flipping Tables	84
Friends	94
Identity	102
Business	110
A Dirty Game	120
The Drift	130
A Bad Mix	136
Black and White	142
Humility	156
Forward	164
A Word from God	170
Wilderness	178
Salvation	182
Forgiveness	190
The Return	196
Opportunity	202
Preparing a Table	212
Rhythm, Flow, Art	222
Purpose	230
Completion	240
Love. Faith. Endurance.	248

Intro

I've been in 3 fights in my life, and I'm not referring to physical battles. In physical fights, wounds heal quickly, but the kinds of fights I've been in can leave one scarred well into old age. The opponents I've fought don't give up. Just when you think you've beaten them, they come back stronger and with better techniques. I've fought to find my true identity, and I've fought to discover the literal meaning of manhood. Each fight taught me lessons that I would never forget. But perhaps the fight with the greatest takeaway, was my fight to exalt my plan over God's.

One thing I've learned about God throughout the years is that He's a gentleman and He's not going to fight with you. Why should He? He's God, and He wants to fight for you. He has plans that are good for us, but often times we get so caught up in pursuing the things that are on our agenda that we don't even consult Him about what He wants for us. So, we go through life facing all kinds of trials and tribulations that we would never have to encounter if we were allowing ourselves to be guided by Him. And that's ok, because God uses those trials and tribulations to shape and strengthen us. But why go through them if you don't have to? See, this relationship with God is based on trust. It all boils down to this question; can we trust this being that we can't see with our lives? Jesus said, "Blessed are they that have not seen, and yet have believed."

On the pages that follow you're going to read a story about a boy that fell in Love with the beautiful game of basketball and placed that game above everyone and everything in his life. And my hope is that you won't make the same mistakes that I did. My hope is that you won't waste any more time and pursue all that is righteous and true. And my hope is that your eyes will be open to the fact that God has placed certain things in our lives not to be worshipped, but to teach us about the one who is to be worshipped.

Desire

"May He grant your heart's desires and make all your plans succeed."
(Psalms 20:4 NLT)

In August of 2016, I was playing professional basketball in Lima, Peru. I just had one of the best performances of my career, although it was in a losing effort. We had a couple days off before it was time to prepare for our next game, so I decided to spend my time catching up on some of the track and field events from the Olympics one afternoon.

The team I played for had made living arrangements with a local family that lived near the team's facility. I stayed there with two other American players, one of which was my best friend, who I played with in college. My room was on the first floor, to the right when you entered the house. It wasn't very big, but it was comfortable. Plus, it was in the perfect location, right next to the kitchen.

The homeowners had an older television inside of a sliding closet that I would open and watch from time to time. All the shows were in Spanish, so I didn't understand them that well. I mainly watched them to pick up the language quicker, but most of the time, I would either watch Netflix on my iPad or read.

I was in Peru during their winter months which lasted from May to September. That was a bit different coming from Georgia where those are our warmest months. The days were pretty much dreary and overcast with a temperature between 50-60 degrees. That afternoon was nice though, around 65 degrees and sunny. As I watched the sprinters,

The Lord gave me something that He had never given me before, an ultimatum. While I sat there, He gently said to me, "You can either stay here and remain the same, or you can follow Me and experience so much more."

That Summer, I had spent a lot of time with God, and I found myself growing closer to Him. I saw my life begin to change, starting with the things that I desired. There were things that I had been engaging in for a while that brought me pleasure, that I no longer wanted to do because they didn't honor God. That summer, I had really given a lot of thought to my purpose and began to search for the exact reason I was created. On my quest, I became a pro basketball player, and was having success doing it. Naturally I began to think this is what I was created to do. But just when I thought I had reached my promised land, The Lord gives me this ultimatum.

The statement He spoke to me might seem vague to some, yet it was anything but to me. In that moment I realized that God's words are life altering because they contain knowledge. One word from Him could set your life on a completely different course. He was telling me that if I continued to play pro basketball I wouldn't grow, but if I walked away, I would experience so much more.

To be a professional basketball player was my life's goal. I remember being four years old and my aunt was making quilts for my brothers and I. She asked us what we wanted to be when we grew up because she was going to incorporate that into the design of the blankets. I told her I was going to be a basketball player and she stitched a basketball onto it. From that point on, every time I saw that patch, it reminded me of my goal. But now I had achieved that goal, yet God was asking me to walk away from it. What would you do?

Don't answer that. I know some are thinking, "I'd be bold in my faith and trust God!" But I've come to realize that you never know what you're going to do in a situation until you're right in the middle of it.

I grew up in Decatur, Ga and like I stated earlier, for me, becoming a professional basketball player was always the goal; and when you set a goal that lofty, you're bound to have few people come around and tell you that you can't do it. Fortunately, I never believed that. I always knew that I would make it, I just didn't know how. Nor did I know what I would have to go through to get there.

All my life, I felt an emptiness inside of me. I knew something was missing, and no matter what I did, I was never able to fill that void. From a young age, I battled thoughts that told me I wasn't good enough and that I would never be good enough. A large part of me believed that, but my aim was to be one of those people that did something that mattered; Even though I wasn't sure what that looked like for me, basketball made sense.

I remember being a young boy playing basketball in my backyard. At that time, it was just a game, something I did for fun, and that's all I saw it as. My view of basketball didn't change until I went to a men's league game my Dad was playing in one night. It was my first time being in a gymnasium and the second I walked in I was captivated by the atmosphere. It was loud, but I didn't care; The combination of grown men yelling and basketballs ricocheting off the floor sounded like a symphony to me. And let's not forget perhaps, the sweetest sound of them all, the ball going through the net. The smell of polyurethane covering the hardwood floor was a bit weird, but later in my life it would become intoxicating.

That night I sat at the baseline holding my Dad's Wilson Jet basketball and watched him and the other adults play for hours, though it felt like minutes. I still remember what he was wearing: a blue 1996 Team USA Olympic Jersey (Hakeem Olajuwon), red shorts, a pair of white Shawn Kemp Reeboks, and his gold chain. That night was my official introduction to basketball, and it was as if a door had been opened to a world that I never knew existed. Basketball was just a game to me at that point, but it would quickly become my desire.

Role Play

"So whether you eat or drink, or whatever you do, do it all for the glory of God."

(1 Corinthians 10:31 NLT)

On every basketball team that I've been a part of, every player has a had a role. Some players were there because they could score, and some players were there because they were great defenders or rebounders. On the really good teams that I've been on, everyone has understood and accepted their role. Everyone might not have liked the role they had, but they understood it and accepted it. I viewed family the same way. The only way families work, is if everyone understands and accepts their given role.

I was fortunate enough to grow up in a two-parent household, and I wouldn't understand how much of a blessing that was until I was in my twenties. My parents were very different people but had similar core values. From a young age I noticed that my Mom, Wanda or Gail, as everyone calls her, was extremely into God. There were times where I would be walking through the house and see her praying and praising God, and she would be crying. I would run up to her and ask, "Mom, what's wrong?" She would laugh and say, "Nothing honey", and then go back to praising Him. I was too young to truly understand her passion for God. She would wake up early and read her Bible at the living room table while drinking her coffee and would always be listening to a pastor on tv or have some sermon playing. Even in her car, the only thing she listened to was Gospel music. For a while, I didn't think she knew that there were other types of shows and music that she could watch and listen to; But then I started to realize that she was truly dedicated to living her life for God. I remember being a child and I would hear her creep into our room early in the morning. She would place her hands on our heads and pray for us as we slept. I can't speak for my brothers, but I know it scared me the first few times it happened and I kind of fought in it a way. Then I realized that she wasn't going to stop, so I just let her do it. Even before bed she would read us Bible stories. Many of the stories I enjoyed and was able to understand and follow along with. Matter of fact, my mom taught me how to read from a book of prayers. I didn't know it at the time, but she was planting spiritual seeds in us. My mom told me that there have only been two times when she's heard The Lord audibly speak to her, and both times were regarding me. The first time He said, "Teach him My Word." And the second, "Let him play basketball." In our family, I saw my mom as The Spiritual Liaison, our direct connection with God.

My dad was a spiritual person as well, but I didn't view him as the spiritual liaison. I saw him as The Enforcer. Growing up, I was terrified of him, but not because he was abusive or anything; I just knew that he didn't play. I can honestly say that every time my dad disciplined me, I deserved it. I was a mischievous kid, and I was always getting into something. He had a green Ford F-150, and whenever I saw that truck pull up to the school, I knew that it was trouble for me. He was a no-nonsense kind of guy; He knew how to have fun, but was all about handling business. Growing up, when things didn't work out the way I wanted them to, he didn't make excuses as to why it didn't happen; He would often say, "that wouldn't have happened if you would have been handling your business." As a kid it seemed harsh, but that was the kind of Love I needed. His father was a military man, so those traits were passed down to him and he held my brothers and I to high standards. He never allowed us to take shortcuts because he knew that the cold world that he and my mom were raising us in wouldn't allow it either.

One of the traits that I've always admired most about my dad was the fact that he was never the kind of person to bite his tongue. If there was something that needed to be said, Clifford Dawson Jr. was going to say it. He didn't care if you agreed with him or not. That was a trait that I wasn't born with but would have to learn. When I started playing basketball there were times when our relationship was rocky because of the way that he pushed me. I remember being at a tournament in Indiana when I was fourteen and him making me run in the parking lot of our hotel because I had a bad game. At times, I just wanted to be a kid and do what other kids were doing like hang out and play video games; But he was looking at the entire picture, while I could only see a small portion of what was going on. He wouldn't allow me to sell myself short, no matter how bad I wanted to at times.

My younger brother Josh and I were polar opposites. I was a basketball player and had a bit of a calmer approach and he was a football player and had more of an "in your face" type attitude. Growing up with personalities that different, we clashed regularly. I guess it was your typical sibling rivalry. But for all the times we clashed, the Love we had for one another abounded much more. Josh looked up to me, and although he was two years younger than me, I found that I was always learning something from him. I watched him win two state championships in High School and then go to the University of Georgia and win the SEC East championship in 2012, his freshman year. He knew how to win, and I viewed him as The Winner. Not only did he know how to win on the field, but he also knew how to win in life. It seemed like everything he did, he was successful in, even though he didn't always realize it.

My brother Nick was two years older than me and four years older than Josh. We had different mothers, but we never viewed him as our half-brother. He was just our brother. We Loved it when he would come to stay with us on weekends. Nick was a musician and extremely confident in his abilities. His confidence was one of the things I admired most about him. Another thing that I Loved about him was the fact that he was going to be who he was everywhere that he went. He Loved to perform, and that's why I viewed him as, The Performer. No matter where he went, he was always looking to put on a show. Some people would shy away from the spotlight, but not Nick; he embraced it.

Growing up, I realized that I was able to define everyone else's role, but I could never clearly establish a role of my own. My role seemed to be constantly changing. I've always had the mindset to just be whatever my family needed me to be. I think being able to play more than one role in the family, eventually translated to basketball allowing me to play more than one position on the court. It's funny how all aspects of your life are connected like that. All I knew is that I Loved these people, and I wanted to protect them. These were the people that God chose to accompany me on this journey called life, and I was willing to do whatever it took to keep them safe because I knew that each of them would do the same for me.

Hope

"Let us hold tightly without wavering to the hope we affirm, for God can be trusted to keep His promise."

(Hebrews 10:23 NLT)

As my interest in the game grew, I began to not only play basketball but watch it also. This was the late 90's and early 2000's so I became familiar with names like Michael Jordan and Kobe Bryant. I remember watching Kobe do things in games and then going outside and trying to imitate those very moves.

My dad informed me that we were related to NBA all-star Latrell Sprewell, and he instantly became my favorite player. I watched him play whenever he was on tv, I got a jersey, and yes, when his shoes came out with the spinning wheel, I had a pair. My dad also told me we were related to WNBA all-star and gold medal Olympian Ashja Jones. He had me watch her along with other WNBA players because they were so fundamentally sound.

Finding out I was related to two professional basketball players inspired me. These were people in my family, people that shared the same blood as me, who had gotten to a place that I could only dream of being. That let me know that it was achievable. But even though I was inspired by both of them, neither one of them inspired me like Sharice.

My brothers, my neighbor, and I were in the backyard playing basketball one day when we saw a group of girls walking up the hill. One yells out to us, "Can we come over?" They were around our ages, and had just moved into the neighborhood. I yelled back, "Let me go check with my mom!" My mom gave me the ok and came outside to meet them. There were four of them altogether, and most of them only cared to do things that most girls their age wanted to like jump rope, pick flowers, and things like that. But Sharice was different. Sharice wanted to play basketball.

Up to that point, I had never seen a girl play the way she played. All the girls at school couldn't even dribble, let alone get the ball to the rim. But not Sharice, she was dribbling between her legs, behind her back, and her jump shot was like water. But her skill on the court wasn't the only thing that made her stand out. She carried herself as if she wasn't afraid of anything, the slim scar under her eye reflected that. As we played in the backyard that day, I fell in Love, not only with her, but she made the game that much more appealing to me. It's hard to put into words my affinity for basketball and Sharice. At the time, the two were almost synonymous in my life. I think this poem will help better explain:

She wasn't the girl next door,
She actually stayed four houses down.

She had braids,
A chipped tooth,
And her skin was almond brown.

A girl that could play basketball was like a unicorn,
I didn't know such a thing could exist.
I was in the second grade,
While she was in the sixth.

All the girls I knew wanted to jump rope and play hopscotch,
But not Sharice.
She was on the basketball court,
Whether it was rain, sleet, cold or hot.

She Loved the game,
Her handles were so tight it was as if the ball was tethered t
her soul.
Her passion for the game inspired me,
Not one, but two-fold.

When Sharice comes to mind,
I think about the story that Common once told,
"I met this girl when I was ten years old,
And what I Loved most, she had so much soul…"

Sharice and I weren't super close or anything, but interacting with her and watching her play did something to me. She enjoyed the game. It was nourishing to her, and it was almost as if she drew strength from it. Observing her relationship with basketball added to the hope that I had for myself with the game.

Fear

The Lord is my light and my salvation; whom shall I fear? The Lord is the strength of my life; of whom shall I be afraid?"

(Psalm 27:1 KJV)

I spent the first eight years of my life in Decatur, Ga. Decatur was home to me, and I Loved everything about it. Our neighborhood was filled with kids, so we'd just run up and down the street all day playing everything from basketball, football, riding bikes and scooters. We would even have all the kids come over and play video games at our house. For an eight-year-old kid like me, that was Heaven. But that's all I could see. I couldn't see the underlying issues that were arising right before me. Let me rephrase that, it's not that I couldn't see them, I had just grown so accustomed to them that they didn't bother me.

It seemed as though there were always gun shots in my neighborhood. There was one incident where bullets came through our home. Having to hit the floor when we heard gun shots was almost a weekly occurrence. It became so routine that it felt like a drill; After the gunshots, my brothers and I would just go back to doing what we were doing like nothing happened. This was becoming "normal" to us. I remember being outside with my dad cutting the grass one Sunday evening. We had been working for a couple hours and there was only a small part left to complete. He told Josh and I to go on in the house while he finished up the last of the work. We lived across the street from the elementary school that we attended and as I entered the house, I noticed that there were cars gathering in the parking lot of the school. A few minutes later shots rang out. We hit the floor, then I heard my dad beating on the door and yelling, "Let me in! Let me in!" My mom crawled to the door to open it for him as the shots were still being fired. I saw jokes on television shows about things like this, but we were really living it, and my parents weren't laughing like the people on tv.

That only seemed to be the beginning of the decline of our neighborhood. The Dekalb County Sheriff, Derwin Brown, lived right around the corner from us and was murdered in his driveway. He was just forty-six years old. From that point on, cops were always rolling though the neighborhood. Again, it seemed normal to me, but that shouldn't be the norm for anyone.

During this time, there was a shift with me. I started to see "people" in our home. There were times where I would see a person or multiple people walking through our living room, and I would run to tell my parents; but when they came, they weren't able to see them. This happened often, and I started to think that I was going crazy. I could see that it frustrated my dad, but my Mom knew exactly what was going on. God was opening my spiritual eyes and I was beginning to see into the spirit realm. There were also times where I would hear someone call my name. I thought it was my parents so naturally I would go to them, but when I got there, they informed me that they hadn't called me. This happened often. One day my mom told me that it was The Lord who was calling me. I wouldn't understand what she meant until years later when I read the story of the prophet Samuel in The Bible, who The Lord called in a similar way.

One Sunday night, I was lying in the bottom bunk of our bunk bed; Normally I slept at the top but I had gotten bigger than Josh so my parents thought it would be safer if I took the bottom, which I absolutely hated. My mom was lying in the bottom bunk with me watching tv. Her plan was to stay there until we fell asleep and then she'd go back in her room with my dad, as usual. But this particular evening I remember turning to face the wall to go to sleep and when my eyes met the wall, there was a pair of eyes looking right back at me. These eyes were red, menacing, and full of hate. There was also a deep darkness around those eyes. I started to freak out, crying and screaming. The fear that fell on me was like nothing I had ever experienced before. My mom took me into her room with my dad. As I was lying in the bed, I saw a tall, dark figure standing at the door. It was taller than the door frame. I saw its eyes were fixated on me and realized that it was the same creature from my room. It was almost like it was following me. I put the covers over my head and cried myself to sleep that night. I would later piece together that I had seen a demon.

Up to that point, I enjoyed being able to see things that other people couldn't, but not after that night. If seeing demons was a part of God's call for my life, I didn't want any part of it. So, I sent God to voicemail and my spiritual eyes were closed for quite some time after that.

I grew up going to World Changers Church International under the leadership of Pastor Creflo Dollar. My mom would listen to him on the radio while on her way to work. One day he was teaching on The Book of Revelation and the end times, and it prompted her to come and hear him speak. She went to one of the Wednesday night services and the rest was history. Her and my dad started attending regularly and would soon come to call the church home. My mom would tell me that when she was pregnant with me and they would go to church, I would jump uncontrollably in her womb when Pastor Dollar would preach. Subsequently I always felt at home or safe when I was there.

World Changers Church is what most people would call a "megachurch" because it had so many members and such a large campus. When you grow up going to a church like that, you don't look at it as a megachurch, you just see it as church; But people didn't view it that way. I soon began to see that people liked the fact that Pastor Dollar taught on prosperity and grace, but they didn't like the fact that he lived a prosperous and graceful life. It didn't make sense that people thought it was ok for a doctor, lawyer, or an athlete to live well, but not a preacher. I always saw preachers as the people who were doing God's work, and if anyone deserved to live prosperously, it was them. And I get it, there have been some pastors who have used The Word of God for personal gain, but not Pastor Dollar. Everything he taught was straight out of The Bible. I remember hearing all kinds of crazy things about him on the news as a child. Things like he was stealing money, or you couldn't be a member of the church unless you made a certain amount of money. None of it made sense to me, and every time he was investigated, he was cleared of all allegations; But I remember seeing the looks on people's faces when we told them what church we went to. Those looks made me afraid to tell people what church I attended and even made me nervous to speak about God.

That fear and nervousness began to spill over into other areas of my life as well. For as long as I can remember, I've felt fear. I always considered what could go wrong instead of what could go right. I often wondered when this started, and I believe that I've pinpointed the exact moment when fear became a constant in my life. I was on the playground one day in elementary school and I saw there were a bunch of kids doing backflips off the elevated area onto the ground. It looked cool and they made it seem so easy that I just knew that I could do it. I always thought the people that could flip and things like that were so cool. There were lots of kids that could flip in my neighborhood, and I always wanted to be one, but I could never get the mechanics down. I thought jumping off the top of the playground would give me a better chance to complete the flip. I climbed up on the playground and observed a few more people take the plunge before I made my move. I stood at the edge of the elevated area, turned around and jumped. I remember feeling so free as I was falling through the air thinking, "I'm actually about to do this." Suddenly, those thoughts were interrupted by the top of my head slamming onto the wood chips on the ground. I had landed directly on my neck. I lied on the ground for a second, taking inventory of my bodily functions. I grabbed my neck and moved my arms and legs before jumping up and running off. I was young, but I understood that things could have gone terribly wrong that day.

    Some people might have seen that incident as a kid just falling off the playground, but it made me think that taking risks were synonymous with danger. I never tried to flip again, and from that point on, I carefully examined everything that I did. That incident made me extremely danger conscious, so much so that I would rarely consider the rewards of taking risks.

    Even though I was a kid, I saw that fear had crippling effects.

Other kids in my neighborhood would walk around the corner and go to the candy lady's house and buy snacks. With me being afraid that something bad could happen on the voyage, I never went. My friends would come back with honey buns, lollipops, and candy bars and I would just be there wishing that I had the courage to make the trip with them.

There were times that I looked at my brothers with envy because they were fearless. They would climb trees, jump off the top of elevated areas without fear of injury, and ride their bikes and scooters down the big hill extremely fast. I opted for the more cautious approach downplaying things that I really wanted to do to make myself seem cooler and not afraid. Other kids would even challenge me to play one on one, but I didn't think I was good enough and I was afraid of losing, so I often declined their invitations.

When I would think about my future self, I saw me as being this big and strong guy who would take on any challenge that came his way. But my fears were quick to remind me that I wasn't that, and that I might not ever be him. I could clearly see who and what that I wanted to be, but fear was standing in my way. Fear was blocking my access to the bridge that would allow me to get to the place that I wanted to get to and become who I wanted to be.

Respect

"Give to everyone what you owe them: If you owe taxes, pay taxes; if revenue, then revenue; if respect, then respect; if honor, then honor."
(Romans 13:7 NIV)

With this newfound fear attached to me, I gave more thought to the things that were happening in my neighborhood. I once considered the gunshots to be normal, now they were traumatizing. Every time I heard anything that remotely sounded like a gunshot, I would tuck my tail and hide. My entire mindset had been changed and I felt as though I was a slave to fear. The only things that seemed to bring me peace was watching cartoons and playing basketball. As a child, I would stay up as late as I could watching cartoons and stay outside playing basketball as long as my mom would let me. That was my way of combatting the fear.

With our neighborhood still on the decline, my parents believed that it wasn't the best environment to raise three young impressionable boys in, and decided it was best that we move. Our neighbors, The Lawrence's, had moved and it tore me up. Their son, Tim, was our best friend in the neighborhood. We would always be at each other's houses, and when they moved so suddenly, I was crushed. This is when I learned that I disliked change. I'm one of those, "if it ain't broke, don't fix it" kind of guys. But you can't stop change, it's inevitable. People change, situations change, and oftentimes there's nothing that we can do about it.

"Decatur where it's greater", is a phrase that I heard growing up my entire life; Subsequently I didn't think there were any other cities greater than Decatur, but now my parents wanted to move. Decatur was home, and I didn't understand it. I had made so many memories there, and now I had so many questions. We lived directly across the street from my school, where would we be going to go to school now? Every Friday we would get Chinese food at Imperial of China on Covington Highway, now where were we going to get Chinese food? But regardless of the questions that I had or how many tears I cried, my parents' minds were made up.

We probably searched for a house for about a year. I remember my parents putting us in the car and taking us to every house that they wanted to view. I guess our opinion kind of mattered since we'd be living there too. We viewed houses late in the evening, early in the morning, and all throughout the weekends. Our Saturdays were non-existent during this time, but we got to see some nice houses. There were about four houses that really stood out to me during this process.

One house was nice, but I saw a snake in the backyard and sprinted to the car, so that was a big no for me. As a kid, I had a fascination with track lights, and one of the last houses we toured had them and I wanted to live there solely because of that. There was another house that was owned by an older couple that really grabbed my attention. There was a blueberry tree in the backyard that they let my brothers and I grab a few from it; I thought that was going to be the one for us because my parents were fond of it too. Then there was a house that we looked at on a Saturday. It was down at the bottom of a steep driveway where there was a lot of land and trees. You literally couldn't see the house from the street because of all the trees. The house was built in the sixties, but it had been recently renovated. The kitchen was bigger than the kitchen of the house we were currently in; There were also more bedrooms, more bathrooms, and did I mention more land. It was in Tucker, GA, which was about fifteen minutes from Decatur, but a safer community. Like many of the other houses that we saw, this house checked off all the boxes, but there was something different about this one. From the moment I walked in, I knew this house was going to be the one. It just felt like home. I felt so much peace in there. I'm not going to lie, I had a rotten attitude during the entire house hunting process because I didn't want to leave Decatur, but when I walked in there, all my reservations disappeared. My parents felt the same way and put an offer in not long after. God must have really wanted us to have that house because my parents put an offer in that was forty-thousand dollars below the asking price and the sellers accepted. We were Tucker bound.

Life in Tucker wasn't that much different from life in Decatur. The biggest change was the environment. We could now play outside and not have to worry about drive-by shootings or the cops always rolling through the neighborhood. Oh, and bullets weren't coming through our house either. Our new neighborhood wasn't filled with kids like our old one, which took some getting used to, but we managed. We would just have to be more intentional about inviting friends over. But being in this new environment really helped bring my mom peace. She was relieved that she didn't have to worry about us getting shot or some drug dealer saying something to us every time we stepped outside to play basketball.

Perhaps the thing that I Loved the most about our new home, was the fact that we had a basketball court in our driveway. It was concrete and a huge upgrade from the patch of dirt court we played on in the backyard of our previous home. This is where I really started to fall in Love with the game. I would go outside to play ball as soon as the sun rose, and I would stay out there well after it set. I would sit around watching basketball on tv with my family. During the summer, watching the NBA playoffs together was almost like a pastime of ours. I remember watching The Lakers battle The Kings in the 2002 Western Conference Finals. Vlade Divac tapping the ball out to Robert Horry to hit the winning shot in game four is an image that will forever be engraved into my mind; right next to Sharice dribbling between her legs as she walked up the hill to go play on the outdoor courts at the school. I was starting to see how beautiful basketball was. I admired guys like Tracy McGrady, Kobe Bryant, and Paul Pierce. They made the game look easy. They made the game look fun. At the time I was looking for a shelter or refuge of some sort, and basketball became that. I didn't see any harm in basketball, and I was enamored with the purity of the game.

Living in a new city meant going to a new school, and a new school meant new friends. I know for a lot of kids, making new friends can be a daunting task, but not for me. My dad has always been the kind of guy that's never met a stranger. He could start a conversation with just about anyone at any time, and I inherited that same gift. Some call it 'the gift of gab', but to me, it was just not being afraid to talk to people. At my new school, Smoke Rise Elementary, I bonded with quite a few kids over basketball. Many of us had different backgrounds, but it didn't matter; I noticed that the game had the power to bring people together, no matter what their upbringing was like.

Up to this point, I had only played basketball in my backyard or driveway. I had been to a few basketball summer camps, but that was the extent of my experience. My parents saw that my passion for the game was growing and it was time to put me on an organized team. They signed me up to play at Smoke Rise Baptist Church which was about two miles from our house. I was nine years old, and this was my first time playing organized basketball. Until now, I thought I was a pretty good basketball player because I made most of the shots on my goal at home. I was an arrogant child and I thought I knew everything about the game, but in the words of my dad, I would soon realize that what thought I knew about basketball, wasn't enough to fill an ants a**.

I was playing with kids who were around my age, maybe a year or two older, but they had been playing ball since they were probably about five years old. They knew the terminology, the drills, and all the little things. Not having that knowledge made me feel somewhat out of place, but I was too invested into the game emotionally to just fall back because I was a little behind. I just knew that I had to catch up. Simple. That first year was truly a learning year for me. I had some games where I would play well and some games where I didn't. It was a season of inconsistency which would later become the story of my life (don't worry, we'll get to that soon enough). As the season progressed, I realized that what I really wanted from the game of basketball, was respect. I wanted people to know that I could play, and I wanted them to respect my game.

My first year at Smoke Rise Elementary, there were two kids that lived in the neighborhood next to mine and rode my bus, John Peter and Jonathan; Jonathan was actually a twin. They were two years older than me and would constantly find ways to pick on me and the other kids on the bus. We started off joning, but I could feel that these two had a genuine dislike for me. Now, for those who don't know, joning is a game where kids or adults, hurl insults at each other about their clothes, looks, families, especially their mothers. Nothing was off limits in this game, and oftentimes they would get the best of me.

No matter how good my insults were, they were never good enough to get them off my back. The situation was challenging, and I couldn't just back down. Ultimately, I just wanted my respect, but I knew that I wasn't going to gain it through joning. I had to do something that would shut them down for good. I had to come up with something that would show them I wasn't one to be messed with. I plotted for weeks hoping to come up with a plan that would break their oppressive rule over the school bus, but nothing came to mind. Then one day I overheard John Peter and Jonathan talking about basketball. I found out that they were playing at Smoke Rise Baptist too and happened to be on the same team. I also found out that they were on our schedule. Then it hit me, basketball was how I was going to beat them.

So, at that very moment, I began to mentally prepare myself for that game although it was weeks away. I envisioned everything that I was going to do to them that game to assert my dominance and gain my respect. I would grab rebounds ferociously like Ben Wallace, block shots like Shaq, score like Kobe, and make it all look too easy like Tracy McGrady. When the week of the game rolled around and they realized that they would be playing against my team, they tried to intimidate me. "I hope you know you're going to lose," "We're gonna beat yall by twenty," they both said. Their words wouldn't bear any fruit though. See, they didn't realize that I had been preparing for this game weeks in advance. There was no way we were losing, this was personal.

In basketball, one of the most demoralizing things that can happen to you as a player is to get your shot blocked, especially if your defender happens to emphatically block it. Blocking shots exhibits dominance. When game day rolled around, I didn't have a lot of points, but I had a lot of rebounds, and a lot of blocks. I had to have blocked their shots at least three times each. I wanted them to know that they would no longer be treating me the way they did. I wanted them to know that I was the dominant one. Whenever either of them put up a shot in my vicinity, it was quickly halted by the palm of my left hand; And when the final buzzer sounded, my team came away with the win.

After the game, I stopped and talked to John Peter and Jonathan. They both congratulated me on the win and a well-played game. I told them, "All I want is my respect," to which Jonathan quickly replied, "you got it man, you definitely have your respect." I felt like Paul Walker in the first Fast and Furious movie when he pulled up to the car meet and stated that if he won the race, he wanted the cash and the respect. Then he went on to emphasize that the respect was more important to him. That part of the movie resonated with me because ultimately that's all I wanted too. Respect was the most important thing to me, and this was the first time I had to fight for mine, but it surely wouldn't be the last.

That day I was starting to see that people will not only like you if you're good at basketball, but they'll also respect you. Another thing that I realized is that the basketball court was the perfect place for me to express myself. Off the court, I wouldn't say too much, nor would I ever show how I truly felt about certain situations, but on the court, I could let my hair down. There were so many feelings that I kept dammed in the reservoir of my heart, mainly feelings of anger. Oftentimes I would forget they were there because I couldn't find a place to safely release them. There just never seemed to be an appropriate time; but on the basketball court, I could open the floodgates.

I would go on to play two more years at Smoke Rise Baptist Church. Each year I was better than the last. In my third year, I was about six feet tall and more skilled than everyone else, and the game was too easy. But although I was progressing, I wasn't being challenged. My dad saw that and realized that some of the things that were working for me wouldn't work on the next level. I had learned as much as I could playing in that league. It was time to find stronger competition.

Leaders

"Without wise leadership, a nation falls; there is safety in having many advisers."

(Proverbs 11:14 NLT)

My Dad is a huge Atlanta fan. It doesn't matter what team it is, Falcons, Braves, or Hawks; If they're from Atlanta, he's going to support them. He even showed Love to the hockey team that we had once upon a time, The Atlanta Thrashers. My Dad is originally from Augusta but came here in 1986, fell in Love with the city and never left. He represented Atlanta everywhere he went and was going to let you know about it. He had Atlanta Falcons, Hawks, and Braves season tickets for years. My brothers and I would Love to go with him to Falcons games on Sundays. We would all have our Falcons jerseys on, and we'd pack into his Toyota Celica and make our way down to The Georgia Dome. I can hear my mom yelling at my Dad now, "You can be early to the football game, but barely get to church on time." That always gave me a good laugh.

Sunday games were always fun. We would meet up with my Uncle Fred and his friends and tailgate before the games. Uncle Fred always had the best food: Chicken, sausages, hot dogs, burgers. We'd get full and then head into the stadium around 12:30pm to catch the kickoff. One Sunday, one of Uncle Fred's friends asked my dad if I played basketball. My dad told him that I did, and we were actually looking for a new team to play on. The man called me over and went on to introduce himself. "My name is Coach Tiger and I coach The Atlanta Celtics, have you heard of them?" "No, sir," I replied. "We're one of the top five AAU programs in the country." AAU stood for Amateur Athletic Union, and it was a sports organization that was geared towards the development of young athletes; And the Atlanta Celtics were known for pumping out some of the top talent the game of basketball had ever seen. Perhaps one of the most talented teams they had consisted of guys like Dwight Howard, who is one of the best big men to play in the NBA, Josh Smith, Javaris Crittenton, and Brandon Rush. He went on to invite us to one of their workouts that upcoming week. He and my dad exchanged numbers and we went into the game. As I sat through the game, all I could think about was getting back on the basketball court. It had been a few weeks since I was last on the court with other players, but what I didn't know is that what I was about to walk into would change my life and my perspective of the game forever. Up to this point, I had only known the nice side of basketball. I didn't know how gritty this game could be. Even though I Loved it, and enjoyed playing it, it was still just a game in my eyes; But to some, it was a way of life.

 The following Thursday my dad took me to Adams Park which is where the Atlanta Celtics held most of their practices and workouts. Adams Park was about thirty miles away from our home, so getting there on a weekday was no easy task when you factor in the Atlanta traffic; But I said that I wanted to play, so my dad was willing to make the sacrifice. The gym had two floors, with the seating upstairs and the court on the lower level. It kind of gave off an arena vibe because on the court you could look up and see people in the stands, which I thought was cool. It was hot and muggy and was filled with kids of different ages, from about ten to fifteen years old. The coaches had them doing drills in various stations throughout the gym. My dad spotted Coach Tiger and he instructed me to get loose and hop in one of the drills.

I scanned the gym as I took my time taking off my sweatpants and putting on my shoes. They had a station where they were doing ball handling, another station for agility, another for defense, and another for shooting. Coaches were yelling, whistles were blowing, sneakers were squeaking against the floor, and the kids were going hard. I had never been in a basketball workout with that level of intensity, and honestly, I was a bit intimidated. From the second I got out there, I could tell that this was a different level and that I was back at the bottom of the totem pole. All the respect I had garnered in the church league meant nothing out here. But this is what I needed. The level that I had been playing on wasn't a true representation of the game of basketball. It was merely an introduction, and this would serve as my wakeup call. I struggled through the workout that night, and my dad knew it. On the way home he asked me, "You sure this is what you wanna do?" "Yes sir, it is," I replied. I was scared. I saw how much further ahead of me those kids were and it really made me consider if this was the route that I wanted to take. Even some of the younger kids were more developed than me, but I wasn't going to stop coming back. I wanted to play ball, and quitting wasn't my style.

My parents were sacrificing a lot for me to play AAU basketball, and I'm not just referring to monetary sacrifices either, even though that was a part of it. But it was more of their time and energy. My dad was a logistics supervisor and worked long hours five to six days a week; And my mom was an accountant who had a demanding schedule as well. I remember us being a few weeks into my time with the Celtics, and we already had a tournament or two under our belts. I was playing ok, but it was apparent that I was still getting adjusted to that level of play. One Sunday, we were at practice, and I didn't want to be there. I would have much rather been at home playing PlayStation or taking a nap, and the way I was practicing reflected that. The coaches were getting on me about my intensity in the drills and lack of focus. My mind just wasn't there that day. Well, my dad had seen enough. He pulled me out of practice and took me to the upstairs restroom. He took off one of his Reebok classics and whooped me right there on the spot. I'll never forget what he told me afterwards. "I'm not driving thirty miles both ways for you to come out here and bull**** around. If you gonna play, play!"

 I went back out there and played with a ferocity that I had never played with before all while trying to conceal the fact that I had just gotten a whooping. At the time I didn't understand the sacrifices that not only my parents were making, but my coaches also. Coach Collier St. Clair or "Coach C" as I called him, was a high school coach and would later go on to coach collegiately, and professionally overseas. He knew the game and was perhaps one of the greatest basketball minds I have ever been around. Coach Robert Daniel, "Coach Rob" is what we called him, was an attorney. He was hard-nosed and would let you know exactly what was on his mind, but always maintained his cool. In high school and college, I would spend a good bit of time with Coach Rob, and he gave me different ways of viewing the world and life. They both could have been using that time to advance their careers, but they decided to spend it on me (and my teammates). That day, I realized that not only did I have an opportunity to play basketball, but an opportunity to position myself for the future. After that, I never took the game, my parents, or my coaches for granted. Plus, it's no fun getting a whooping at practice.

I grew a lot as a player throughout the course of that initial AAU season. I even became a viable option offensively for us. But it was clear to see that I didn't have the respect I was seeking, and that meant I still had a lot of work to do. I would play AAU for a total of five years, from the time I was twelve, until I was seventeen. During my third year, Wallace Prather, who was the founder of The Atlanta Celtics, passed away and the Celtics were now under new management. Not everyone agreed with the direction they wanted to take the organization. So, what do people do when they have irreconcilable differences? They split, and a new team would emerge, The Atlanta Select, and that's the side of the line we fell on.

For the most part, we still had the same team. The only thing that really changed was the name on the jerseys. For me though, it was a fresh start. The Atlanta Celtics had so many great players come through the program, and I felt that lots of us would be playing in their shadows. But with the Select, we had a chance to start something of our own. We had an opportunity to put our names on the map, and that's just what we did. And honestly, I felt a lot more connected to the city wearing that red and black, opposed to the green and gold. This was around the time, I really started to get a feel for the game of basketball, and I was shaping up to be a solid player. I was about 6'2, I was dunking, my footwork was getting better, and my jump shot was coming around too. Fun fact, I was the first player to ever put on an Atlanta Select uniform.

Playing AAU were some of the best times of my life. We traveled all over the country and played some of the best players. I remember playing against Brandon Knight when I was fourteen in Orlando. He put up forty-two points on us that night. We had never come across anyone who had that kind of skill. That's why I liked playing against players from different states. It gave me a chance to see what else was out there. It also let me know what I needed to improve on.

Playing against different players was fun, but when I look back, perhaps the best part of AAU for me were the relationships that were formed. During the summers, I spent more time with my teammates than I did with anyone else. We did everything from fight to stay up til 3am playing video games. What I Loved the most about my teammates was that each of us came from a different world, meaning that we all had different experiences and were into different things. My teammates introduced me to new music, television shows, and altogether I was beginning to see different aspects of life just by interacting with them. They were my brothers. But it wasn't just my teammates who I had a close bond with, I viewed my coaches as my older brothers too.

I told you about Coach C and Coach Rob earlier. I have so much respect for these two because when I first came to them, they took a chance and invested in me. They would meet my dad and I at the gym on days when we didn't have practice just to help me get some extra work in. I didn't realize it then, but now I see how great of a sacrifice that was. Coach Rob was an Atlanta Hawks season tickets holder, and as I got older, he would take me to the games quite often. I'll never forget him taking me to see Tracy McGrady play when I was in the ninth grade which was one of the best experiences of my life. He put up 37 points on the Hawks that night. I could trust these guys, and I knew they not only cared about my development as a player, but they wanted to see me grow up and be a good man.

We had two other coaches come in who would also become older brothers and mentors to me, Rahn Gatewood and Sarath Degala. Rahn was an attorney from Memphis, Tennessee. He was about 6'7 and worked with me a lot on my footwork and post moves. He was also one of the smoothest and coolest people I've come across in my life. It never seemed like too much bothered him, a trait that I would soon begin to adopt. Sarath had a very high-ranking position in healthcare and was a sports fanatic. He was about 6'2 and had the most fluent jump shot I've ever seen. I mean, when he shot the ball, it barely touched the rim; A true work of art.

So, we had an all star coaching staff: Coach C, Coach Rob, Coach Rahn, Coach Sarath, and my dad. My dad always found a way to be on the coaching staff of every non-school team that I played for when I was coming up. He knew the game, and coaches respected his views, so they would always ask him to help out. When it came to positive male influences, these were the guys I looked up to and still look up to today. Anytime I had a problem or needed some advice, I could talk to either one of these guys about it. And the funny thing was that it seemed like all of them were saying the same thing to me at the same time; That's how I knew I was dealing with like-minded individuals and that their advice was trustworthy. This super team of role models came together at just the right time in my life. My future seemed extremely bright because I had a front row seat to what real leadership looked like; But even with all this positivity around me, I had no idea that I was about to enter such a dark place.

40 Pills

"For it is by Grace you have been saved through Faith – and this is not from yourselves, it is the gift of God"

(Ephesians 2:8 NIV)

By the time I was in the eighth grade, the shelter that was basketball had now become my home. I felt comfortable on the court, and I finally began to feel as though I belonged; but every day I woke up and put on a mask and pretended to be someone who I wasn't just so I could fit into society. Yet on the basketball court, I didn't need a mask, and I didn't have to worry about fitting in. I could be who I wanted to be. I could actually be Brandon Dawson. I yearned for that kind of freedom in everyday life, but it didn't seem as though it existed.

During the first few weeks of school, I was so excited about the upcoming basketball season that I had neglected some of my school work. Subsequently I ended up with an "F" in science, and I knew that meant my parents weren't going to let me play ball. My parents didn't always agree on everything, but there was one thing they did agree on, and that was school. They didn't even like for us to bring home a "C" so I knew this science grade would cause some problems. I could already hear my dad, "I'm not raising you to be another ni**a standing on the corner!" He would say that every time he felt we weren't doing our best. But believe it or not, I wasn't worried about what my parents would say, I was more upset about possibly not playing basketball. I had fallen in Love with the game. I couldn't imagine being separated from it. I'd much rather die than to not be able to play basketball. To some people, basketball was just a game, but to me it was the only thing keeping me alive. I felt like it was the only thing I was truly good at, and it made me feel like my life was worth something. I mean, I had learned that people not only liked me if I could play this game well, but they would also respect me; and from my findings in my then thirteen years of life, I came to the conclusion that life was a big popularity contest. It was about being liked and respected.

If I couldn't play basketball, it didn't make sense to live. So, I decided that I would kill myself. I know, killing yourself because your parents weren't going to let you play basketball sounds pretty wild, right? But when you're a thirteen-year-old kid who doesn't understand how the world works and the only thing that makes sense and brings you any peace is about to be taken away, what choice do you have?

I've always been the kind of guy that once my mind was made up, there was no changing it; And my decision to go through with this was rooted firmly. For about a week I went back and forth about how my family would feel if I was gone, constantly asking myself, "would they miss me?" I knew they Loved me, and I'm sure they would be sad if I was gone, but the thought that dominated my mind was, "no one is gonna care if what I Love and cherish is taken away, so why should I take their feelings into consideration?"

I had seen tv shows and heard news reports of people killing themselves by overdosing on pain pills. I thought that they would cause me to go to sleep and never wake up, and honestly, that sounded like the most peaceful way to die. This wasn't the first time that I wanted to die though. I remember being a young kid, probably around the age of six or seven, and feeling the same way. I'm not sure what it was, but I just remember feeling as though I shouldn't be living. The feeling was so substantial that there were even times where I would pray to God and ask Him to not allow me to wake up.

There was a bottle of ibuprofen in our kitchen cabinet with five hundred pills in it. Each one being five hundred milligrams. We would grab a couple when someone had a headache or some kind of pain. I began reading the bottle and it said not to take more than six in twenty-four hours. It was a Friday morning, and I took six before I left for school and had a plastic bag with ten more pills that I would take throughout the day. In a last effort cry for help, I told my friends that they weren't going to see me on Monday, because I was going to die that weekend. "Shut up man! Stop playing!" They thought that I was joking. It hurt that they couldn't see that I was begging for help, but in that moment, I realized that no one was coming to save me. I felt helpless and alone, and following through with this act made even more sense.

Throughout the day I consumed the ten pills I brought to school, and when I got home, I took twenty-four more to make it an even forty. I don't know why I stopped at forty or why that number was even in my head. I thought that I would just drop dead right there in the kitchen, but I felt fine. I went outside to play basketball, thinking that this would be my last time playing the game that I Love. I stayed out there for an hour or so before heading in. Still feeling fine, I proceeded to do everything I would normally do on a Friday night in middle school, like eating Chinese food and playing video games.

The next day I woke up, still feeling well. I thought, "Maybe the pills were expired. Maybe they don't have any effect on me." My younger brother Josh, who was eleven years old at the time, had a football game that afternoon. I Loved going to his games for two reasons. The first reason was I Loved watching him play. The second reason was the French fries from the concession stand! At those games, if I could watch him play and spend a dollar and get an order of fries, I was good. My dad was going to meet us at the game so my mom, josh and I got ready at the house. I grabbed a Little Debbie snack cake, swiss cake rolls to be exact, to eat while I waited for everyone to finish getting ready. Immediately after I finished eating, I had to vomit. Then a slight headache came on. I told my mom I wasn't feeling well and couldn't go to the game. Then I went to lie down. They came back a few hours later with an order of fries for me from the game, but I was so sick, just looking at them made me nauseous. Mom cooked hot dogs and chili that night with homemade fries, which was one of my favorite meals at the time. She would toast the buns, making them perfectly brown and crispy. But it didn't matter to me, I couldn't keep any solid food down. The only thing that I could eat were saltine crackers and ginger ale.

I woke up the next morning and my condition had worsened. In addition to the vomiting and headache, my stomach was on fire. My mom called my dad, who was at work, to let him know that she was taking me to the hospital. Back in 2005 when all this was going on, we didn't have smartphones with GPS, so we had to use MapQuest. My mom got on the computer and printed directions to the nearest hospital. On the ride, we stopped at a red light in front of Tucker High School, and I opened the door and vomited all over the street and the side of my mom's brand-new Dodge Durango. Fun times.

We got to the hospital, and they had us waiting in the emergency room for what seemed like hours. When we finally got to see a doctor, I remember them saying that I was extremely dehydrated and hooking me up to an IV. After that, I was in and out of sleep for the next three days. Whenever I woke up, there were two things that were constant; The first thing was that one of my parents were always there. I was never alone. As I reflect on this situation, I think God allowed it to get to the point it did because He wanted me to see that I was Loved. Years later He would reveal to me just as my parents didn't leave my side during that situation, He would never leave my side either. The second thing was that it rained continuously. This was during the time of Hurricane Katrina, one of the worst natural disasters to ever hit America. I went to New Orleans in 2019 for Jesse Duplantis' Visionary Conference and just about every local I met mentioned to me something about Katrina and how they were still recovering from it fourteen years later.

As I was slipping in and out of consciousness, I thought to myself, "I don't want to die. Not here. Not like this." The doctors had been running tests and concluded that there had been some damage done to my liver, taking forty ibuprofen pills will do that to you, and I had a form of hepatitis. I was getting better though, and after that Wednesday, I was finally healthy enough to go home.

When I got home, I had no desire to live. Even though I had seen how my parents faithfully sat and slept in uncomfortable chairs for days and ate bad hospital food with me, I still didn't feel like I was worthy of their Love. My parents were warriors, prepared to do whatever it took to get the job done, and their son was a coward. I was a scared little boy. I was weak, and they were strong, and I didn't see how I could ever make them proud. I decided that I was going to try to kill myself again and rid my family of this weakness.

Grandma Pansy was my Mom's mom, and lived in Decatur. When we were kids, she would keep us during the summers along with my Aunty Dot. Grandma Pansy didn't have cable, so we watched all the local channels and whatever she was watching. In the afternoon, she would have the tv on her stories. She was a big fan of Days of Our Lives and would watch it every day at one o'clock. I can hear her coming in the room now, "Ok you two, it's time for me to watch my stories."

After Grandma's stories went off, it was time to watch the news. From a young age, I noticed that watching the news will have you afraid to go outside. All they ever reported were the bad things that were going on. "This person got shot" and "that person got killed." It was like they were intentionally trying to fill the people with fear. I have never been a fan of the news, but I can't say that I didn't learn a lot of interesting things while watching.

My mom came to pick us up one afternoon around 5:30pm. She sat down and talked with grandma for a second while we gathered our belongings. As I waited for mom to finish her conversation, the news was reporting on a woman who had been accused of killing her husband. She didn't shoot or stab him, she poisoned him with antifreeze. This was so interesting to me because I had seen my dad pour that into a reservoir under the hood of his car. Thinking back to this, I realized that was going to be the way to rid my family of the weakness.

I did some research on the effects of antifreeze on the body before I decided to ingest it for myself. Antifreeze contains ethylene glycol, propylene glycol, and methanol. Some of our foods and other products contain propylene glycol which isn't deemed harmful in small amounts, but ethylene glycol and methanol are extremely dangerous if ingested. A small amount of either of those can do a lot of damage to the human body; but I didn't care, I was just ready for life to be over.

At this point, it wasn't even because basketball might be taken away from me. I felt weak and ashamed. I didn't feel worthy to live. I felt like a failure. I didn't know it at the time, but satan, our enemy, looks for weak spots in our defenses and then exposes them. Back then, one of my greatest fears was to be viewed as weak, and he was beginning to exploit it.

It was a sunny afternoon, a Thursday I believe, and I had finally done all the research that I needed to do. I had made the decision that today would be the day I die. I was home by myself so there was no one there to stop me. I went outside with an empty water bottle and went to the storage closet where we kept the antifreeze. I had to dig through bottles of engine oil and car washing materials before I found what I was looking for. I removed the yellow cap and took a whiff, and to my surprise it didn't really have a smell. I began to pour it into the water bottle, filling it up about a quarter of the way. I looked at the bottle, and I couldn't help but think that I literally had my life in my hands, or so I thought. As much as I didn't want to drink it, I forced myself to put that bottle to my lips. Sip, sip. Gulp, gulp. I stood there for a second, waiting for the inevitable, but what happened next changed my life forever.

I heard a voice. This voice was almost like a whisper. It spoke to me in a tone that was calm, yet authoritative. "I'll never let anything happen to you." I looked to my left, right, front, and behind, but there was no one there, no one that I could see anyway. I had never heard this voice before, but I knew exactly who it was. Jesus. Those seven words He spoke set me free from suicidal thoughts. I could literally feel the tree of fear that had sprouted being uprooted out of the ground of my heart. I knew that I could trust this voice and I knew that this promise would stand. I poured out the antifreeze, threw the bottle away before walking back in the house, never to feel any effects of the antifreeze ingestion.

    Looks like I was wrong; Someone did come to save me.

Against the Grain

"Don't copy the behavior and customs of this world, but let God transform you into a new person by changing the way you think. Then you will learn to know God's will for you, which is good and pleasing and perfect."

(Romans 12:2 NLT)

I was able to get my grades up and my parents agreed to let me play basketball my eighth-grade year, and I experienced all sorts of success. I finished as the top player in DeKalb County, I was invited to the Adidas Phenom 150 camp in San Diego, CA that summer, and I was rounding out to be quite the versatile player. Towards the end of the school year, James Hartry, the Head Coach for the varsity team at Tucker High School, came down to the middle school to invite me to camp with their team in a few weeks. Everything seemed to be falling into place for me.

There was only one problem. I was what you called silently defiant. I wasn't one to cause a scene or get rude, I would just do what I wanted to do. No one could tell me anything, and I thought that my way was always right; That's sometimes the problem when you experience "success" early on in life. When it came to Brandon Dawson, no one knew what was best for him like Brandon Dawson did, and you couldn't convince me otherwise (some people would argue that nothing has changed). I was hardheaded and I didn't like doing things the conventional way. If everyone else was doing something a certain way, I made it a point to be different. I would always find a way to stand out, and oftentimes it didn't take that much to do it. I've found that sometimes subtlety is the best quality. If we were going through drills and coach said spin to the middle and shoot a hook, I would spin to the middle and throw a shoulder fake in there, then shoot the hook. I think I was so "defiant" because I was afraid. I was afraid of losing my independence and freedom and not becoming who I wanted to be. I had already felt as though I was wearing a mask and not being true to myself; The defiance was my last attempt to be who I truly was.

I remember falling while playing as a child. I would get little cuts and scrapes and my Mom would always put a bandage on them and kiss them for me. A couple days later when it would start to heal, I would notice that a scab was beginning to form, and she would tell me, "Don't pick the scab or it'll leave a scar." I would always pick the scab, and most of the time it did leave a scar. But I was curious, and I needed to find answers on my own. That curiosity was often mislabeled as defiance, which ultimately developed into an against the grain mindset for me. I started to notice that when I did things the way that I wanted to do them I got results. Which in turn plunged me deeper into the pool of exploration and pushed me even harder to live life on my terms.

For as long as I could remember I've never been one to follow the crowd, and I think it started when I was in the first grade. All the "cool kids" had Jordan's, and they would clown anyone who didn't have a pair. Back then I was wearing Nike's, but Nike's weren't Jordan's, so I was subject to getting clowned as well. For months I begged my dad for a pair and finally one Saturday he took me to the mall to pick up the coveted shoes. They were the black and red Jordan 12's, better known as the "Flu Games" because of the performance Jordan had while wearing them and experiencing flu like symptoms. I couldn't wait to wear them on Monday.

When I got to school that Monday, I sat at the table with the cool kids and said, "guess who got a pair of Jordan's this weekend!" with the biggest smirk on my face as I leaned back in my seat. They all quickly looked under the table to check my footwork. I was expecting them to congratulate me; But instead of congratulating me, Deja said in her New York accent, "Son, you got on the old Jordan's!" Then everyone started to laugh. See, what I didn't realize was that the Jordan 13's had come out. I sat there confused as everyone laughed because although I had Jordan's, they weren't the newest pair, so I wasn't considered cool. In a moment of clarity, I decided that I would never again try to keep up with the crowd; Instead, I would go against the norm and do my own thing, even if people didn't fully understand it.

Years later my dad took me to Suwaunee Sports Academy to watch some of the top high school players compete in the Adidas Superstar Camp. Future NBA players such as Gerald Henderson, Stanley Robinson, and Brooke and Robin Lopez all participated. As we sat down to watch one of the games, my dad pointed out Wayne Ellington, who was the most sought-after player in the camp. He walked out on the court with extreme confidence, and I could feel it radiating off him. You could tell there was no doubt in his mind that he was going to dominate that game. But although his confidence was so thick you could cut it with a knife, his shoes stuck out more than anything. They were different than the low-cut blue and white sneakers many of the other participants wore. These were mid-cut, black and white, with some of the wildest designs I had ever seen; And I couldn't take my eyes off them. "Yo Dad, what are those?" I asked as I pointed to the young man's feet. "Oh, those are the Crazy 8's, Kobe Bryant's first shoe," he replied. I was never one to tell my dad what to do, but I looked him straight in the eyes and said, "I gotta have those!" When they released to the public a year later, my parents made sure that I had a pair.

After that, all I wore was Adidas. People would say things like, "get some Nike's!", but I had found what worked for me, which was the premise of me going against the grain. This against the grain style even spilled over into the way I played basketball. I had more of an old school style of play, which I believed helped my game stand out.

I came to the conclusion that the way I lived my life couldn't be based on how everyone else lived theirs, or by doing what someone else thought was best for me. I had to do what worked for Brandon Dawson. Even if it meant being viewed as someone who was defiant or arrogant, that was a hill that I was willing to die on. I saw early on that God hadn't created us to fit in, but we were all created uniquely. The fact that no other person in the history of the world has ever had or ever will have the same fingerprint as me told me everything that I needed to know about life.

Focus

"For as he thinketh in his heart, so is he."
(Proverbs 23:7 KJV)

I had mixed feelings about coming into high school. My middle school teachers made it sound like it was going to be a horrible place where the teachers hated us, there would be fights every day, and police would be constantly in our school searching for drugs and other contraband. Honestly, it sounded like I was going to jail instead of high school.

My mom's red Dodge Durango pulled up on the first day to the front entrance of Tucker High School school. I was surprised to see about six guys from the basketball team standing outside. "Wassup B! Where you been?" they yelled as I got out of the vehicle and made my way up the steps. I had worked out with them during the summer, so they knew who I was, but I had missed the last few weeks of workouts due to traveling with my AAU team. Since I didn't really understand high school, I decided to hang out with them to see how it all worked. From them I learned what to do and what not to do, and from what I observed was that high school was nothing like what my eighth-grade teachers described. Sure, we had some fights and things like that, but for the most part it was pleasant. It was still school; we were just a bit older now.

After a couple weeks of workouts and pickup games after school, there was speculation about me possibly playing varsity my freshman year and I got the feeling that some of the older guys didn't care for that. They didn't come out and say it, but they would say things to get in my head during our morning hangouts. "You played alright yesterday, but those lil moves ain't gonna work during the season." To be honest, I didn't see myself playing varsity my freshman year. I just didn't think that I was consistently able to play on that level yet, and ultimately, neither did Coach Harty. Before tryouts, Coach came to me and let me know that I would be playing JV (junior varsity) and he would look to move me up after the season. I understood the decision and realized that every JV game and practice would serve as an audition for me to get to the next level.

    Coach Lamar was the head coach on JV, the head assistant on varsity, and one of the best coaches I've ever played for. He was the only coach that I've ever had that would actually work out with us; But not only would he workout with us, he would do it in a full sweatsuit and would out work a lot of us. He also had a 1971 Chevy Monte Carlo with the 454 motor. That thing was sweet. I saw Coach Lamar as someone that I could trust. He was a Tucker graduate himself and had literally walked the same halls when he was our age. He knew what we were going through as young men and could relate. During my four years at Tucker there were times that I felt as though I wasn't playing to the best of my abilities and would get down on myself. If I felt like I was underperforming, the weight of the world was on my shoulders, but Coach Lamar always knew what to say to help lighten the load and get me back on track.

    A lot of players who had the potential to be on varsity their freshman year might not have been as accepting of a JV role as I was, but I was thankful to be on JV that year. It was probably one of the most exhilarating seasons of basketball that I've ever played. I felt as though I was becoming more intimate with the game and beginning to see how beautiful basketball really was. And although I was enjoying the game, it acted as a mirror and showed me the strengths and weakness of my game which was a beautiful process.

I remember walking out of the locker room at Dunwoody High School after our last JV game. Coach Lamar stops me just before I get on the bus and says, "Dawson, bring your gear tomorrow. We're moving you up to varsity. It's time to start getting you ready." On the outside I was stoic, but internally I was doing backflips. "Yes sir", I replied. All the work I put in had paid off and I had gotten to the place I longed to be; and fortunately for me, I had an opportunity to be a part of something special.

I arrived at the varsity level with a couple games left in the regular season. The varsity had a record of 25-1, having only lost to rival Columbia High School earlier in the year. This was a state championship contending team and I had a chance to be a part of it. I think I played in maybe three games on our road to procuring a state championship. I didn't play any vital minutes, but I got a taste of what it felt like to play on that level.

On March 9th, 2007, we beat Columbia High School for the AAAA Georgia state championship. I had won a state championship as a freshman, which doesn't happen often. I've been on a lot of teams in my life, but never a team that was as talented as that one. I had gotten a front row seat to see what it took to be a champion; And I saw that it took more than just talent. You have to be willing to do the things that other players and teams just weren't willing to do. Whether it be practicing twice a day, sitting down to watch your mistakes on film, or playing through injuries. I saw that just being talented wasn't enough. You also had to have a coach who you were willing to run through a wall for, and Coach Hartry was that guy. He would do anything for his players; therefore his players would do anything for him. I also realized that I wasn't just there to be along for the ride, I was there to learn; and I would need to learn quickly because now there was a target on my back. My days of being a spectator were over, now I had to perform.

The summer going into my sophomore year was probably the most brutal stretch of basketball that I've ever had to endure in my life. We had lost all but one of our starters from our state championship team, and we had to rebuild. Coach Hartry knew the players that he had didn't have the experience that was needed to be successful that upcoming year. So, he threw us in the fire. All we did was play in summer league games and team camps. Team camps were like tournaments that high school teams would play in during the summer to gain experience and prepare for the upcoming year. We played twenty-one games in eleven days. To give you an idea of how much that is, our high school season was usually about twenty-five games but that spanned over a few months. We played almost that same amount in just under two weeks. My body was exhausted, but I can deal with a tired body. It was my mind that was having trouble finding strength. The game of basketball is seventy percent mental, and I was seeing myself make plenty of mistakes on the court that could have been avoided if I would have just been thinking. I was playing against guys that were a few years older than me and probably better than me at the time. I wasn't as dominant as I had been accustomed to being, and it felt like I was back at the bottom of the totem pole.

A large part of me feeling the way I felt was due to my inconsistent play; One game I would play well, while the next game it looked like I didn't know what I was doing.

We played against Miller Grove High School at Georgia Tech University that summer. I pulled up for a jumpshot that wasn't needed in a crucial part of the game. Coach Hartry calls a timeout and in the huddle, he looks directly at me and says, "You playing like a ho*!" Everyone in the gym heard it. I was embarrassed, but he wasn't wrong. I felt like I could be playing better too. My inconsistencies would follow me into the season as well, which would eventually be compounded by tendonitis in my left knee; Making it hard to run and jump on at times. To top it all off, I was becoming distracted.

Up until this point, basketball was the most important thing to me. Nothing mattered to me like the game, neither did anything bring joy to my life like it. I was always playing basketball and if I wasn't playing it, I was thinking of when my next opportunity to play would be. Don't get me wrong, I held other things in high regard, but basketball sat on the throne of my heart. Yet now, seeds that had been planted long ago were beginning to sprout and would cause disarray in a garden that had been so carefully cultivated.

I remember being around the age of six and going to the mall with my dad and brothers one Friday night after being picked up from my grandma's house. Whenever we went to the mall, the first thing we wanted to do was go to the shoe store. Even if we weren't getting shoes, it was always cool to go in and see what new releases they had so when it was time to get new shoes, we knew what to ask for. We were walking around the store aimlessly when a young lady who worked there asked my dad, "You guys need any help?" in a sweet and seductive voice. "Not right now, we're just looking around" He replied. We continued to look around for a few more minutes before making our way out of the store. As we were leaving, the young lady said to my dad while pointing at me, "You gotta watch this one, he's gonna be the lady's man!" My Dad laughed as we walked out. That might've seemed like a harmless exchange, but the words she spoke over my life that day began to warp my perception of manhood almost immediately.

    I started to notice that the men who were most celebrated in our society were the ones that were athletes or deemed attractive; Subsequently they were the ones who seemed to always have beautiful women at their side. I now paid close attention to those intimate scenes in movies and shows, taking note of the men's actions and words. I took interest in girls while all my friends were too afraid of catching cooties (Can someone please explain to me what cooties are?). I was beginning to think that in order to be considered a real man, you had to be an athlete and you had to always have a girl. This was the distorted view of manhood that I grew up with and I think a lot of our young men are growing up with today.

    Now I was fifteen, and I was emulating the behavior and scenes that I grew up watching and fantasizing about. Sex was fun, and I saw it as more than just a reproductive act. It was another outlet that allowed me to express myself and be who I wanted to be. I was a reserved person who was always putting on an act, but in the bedroom, I could reveal the true essence of who I was; and I was comfortable doing it, even if it was with someone who I barely knew. Often times I enjoyed those encounters the most because there was no expectation for me to act a certain way, they were getting the non-diluted version of me. The version I liked most. At the same time my mom was having these vivid dreams about me with women. "The Lord gave me a dream about you last night Brandon", she would say. Each dream would be symbolic of me having sex. I would just deny it, but my mom was so in tune with God that she knew exactly what was going on; I don't think she was comfortable talking to me about what I was doing though.

There were times where my Love for basketball and sex were at odds, and it was almost as if they were fighting over me. Both were expressive outlets, but it seemed at times that the two were evenly matched; However, I could always tell which one was winning the battle based on my performance on the court.

Eagle's Wings

But they that wait upon The Lord shall renew their strength; they shall mount up with wings as eagles; they shall run and not be weary; and they shall walk, and not faint.

(Isaiah 40:31 KJV)

For years my mom had been waking my brothers and I up at 5:45am to pray before we got ready for school. By the time she woke us up, she had already had a cup of coffee, read her Bible, and been praising God for forty-five minutes herself. She was all in for God, and that was what I admired most about her. Her faith was inspiring, but as I got older, it felt like I was just going through the motions. My prayers were no longer heartfelt, and it seemed like I was doing all of that for my mom, instead of God. See, I knew who God was, but I didn't know Him for myself, and by the time my junior year rolled around, I had wandered far from the path that I was raised on. I felt like I was in a jungle on my own, lost, and had no way of getting home.

I had gotten my license and a 1998 powder blue Mercury Mystique when I turned sixteen, and to me, it might as well have been a Rolls Royce. I took that thing everywhere: school, practice, the mall, and I even took it to a few places I shouldn't have. I knew it was a blessing to have a car of my own at that age, but I didn't understand it, and would soon begin to misuse it. I started picking up different girls and skipping school to go places to have sex. This would be something that happened two to three times a week. The car that my parents bought me as a means of transportation was nothing more than a vessel to satisfy my pleasure, and perhaps the worst part was that I was doing all this while I had a girlfriend.

We met through a mutual friend and had been dating for about a year. Her name was Adrian and was one of the sweetest people that I had ever met. Adrian went to a different school, but she didn't live far from me, so we were able to see a lot of each other. I had dated other girls in the past, but none on the level that she and I were on. Adrian was the first girlfriend that I had who shared her world with me. It was weird to me that someone could be so open about who they were and share their innermost feelings with another person. With me coming from a world of basketball that taught me to be tough and protect myself at all times, I couldn't fathom opening up to someone like that. I was afraid to. With her being so open, it made me feel as though there was something that I was missing, so I searched for it in her; and when I couldn't find what I was looking for in her, I searched for it in other girls.

Adrian knew people that went to Tucker and would often hear about me and these other girls, but I denied it (although it's not a skill that I'm proud of, I was once a masterful liar). With each allegation that arose, I could see a bit of Adrian dying. She thought so highly of me, and it hurt her to see that I wasn't exactly who she thought I was. She was the first person that was able to catch a glimpse under my mask, and I realized that what she saw wasn't attractive to her; And with every tear that fell from her eyes I saw that the person under that mask wasn't so attractive to me either, but I didn't care. The only thing that mattered to me was making sure that I was satisfied. There was something ugly and selfish deep within me, but I was afraid to confront it, nor did I know how. So, I ran from it. My hope was that if I didn't have to confront whatever this thing was, it couldn't affect me.

Just before the season began, I broke my arm. We were playing a pickup game after school one day and it got heated. This year we had a team full of competitors and I knew we had what it took to win another state championship. I believed it so much that I had given my dad my state championship ring that summer and said, "hold this for me, I gotta go get one on my own." Even though I was on the team my freshman year when we won it, I didn't feel as though I had contributed enough to call myself a champion. I just happened to be in the right place at the right time. That afternoon I went up for a dunk in one of the last games of the day and was undercut by a teammate and fell from the air. I put my arm down to brace my fall and the impact caused me to fracture my radius. I knew it was broken the second it happened. I sat on the ground wincing in pain as my teammates gathered around me. I heard a loud voice from across the gym yell, "GET UP!" My dad had snuck into the gym on his way home to watch us play. He hated seeing my brothers and I on the ground. He would always say, "If your leg ain't broke, get up!" I tried to keep playing, but I knew there was nothing I could do and left the gym soon after.

I don't know if I've ever been as angry as I was on that drive home. It felt like all the work I had put in had just went down the drain. I played extremely well that summer during AAU and was now on the radar of a lot of division one college programs that were looking forward to watching me that upcoming season. I was afraid that now they wouldn't get the chance. As I sat at the red light near the ice cream shop up the street from my house, I contemplated wrapping my car around a telephone pole, but I knew that wouldn't solve anything. I walked in the house with tears in my eyes. I just wanted to get to my room, but my mom stopped me in the kitchen. My dad had already told her what happened at the gym. She looked me in my eyes and said, "It's gonna be alright, honey" as she hugged me. Honestly, I didn't believe that it was going to be alright. It felt like my dream of becoming a pro was over. It was already hard enough to get college coaches to take an interest in me, and it seemed as though my opportunity had just slipped through my hands. The tears fell as I melted in my mom's embrace.

Often times when something is taken away from you, you begin to appreciate it more. Basketball was a part of me and now that I wasn't able to play, I felt even more incomplete; and I didn't like the path that I was going down. It was dark, and I was alone. It felt like the only thing I had going for myself was basketball, and without it I was lost. But now that I was on the sidelines in a cast, I could see another side of the game. I knew the game was beautiful and allowed me to express myself in ways that I probably never would have been able to; But now I saw that the game also represented freedom. In between those lines I was free from all the outside noise. Nothing else mattered. But I didn't want that freedom to be limited to the basketball court, I wanted that freedom in my personal life as well. Without basketball I had become depressed and looked for upliftment from sex, but I couldn't find it there. It seemed as though the only place freedom existed for me was in between those lines.

On New Year's Eve 2008, I gave my life to Christ. Pastor Dollar had preached a message on the reality of hell. It was so compelling that it made me examine my own life, and it confirmed what I already knew. I would be going to hell if I didn't make some changes. I wanted to change my eternal destination, but I also wanted relief from everything that was weighing me down while on the Earth. But I felt like I was so far from God, and I couldn't live up to the standard. Ultimately, I didn't think I was good enough, and within a week I was back to doing what I was doing. I left every sexual encounter with a feeling of deep conviction that what I was doing was wrong. I would find myself pleading with The Lord for forgiveness and telling Him that this wasn't the type of lifestyle that I wanted to live, but I wasn't able to pull myself from it. It seemed like no matter how many times I pleaded, I couldn't break the cycle. I was conflicted because deep down I knew what I was doing was wrong, but I felt like this was the only way to achieve true manhood. I had to be the ladies' man, I had to be an athlete, I had to be the man who I saw in movies and television shows.

When I was finally able to get back on the court, it felt like a step in the right direction. My Mom gave me some index cards to read before my games with Bible verses on them. Many of them were verses that I'd heard before about allowing yourself to be strengthened by God and winning the battles that were before you; But there was one that stuck out the most. It was poetic, encouraging, and would later become the verse that was the foundation of my faith:

But they that wait upon The Lord shall renew their strength; they shall mount up with wings as eagles; they shall run and not be weary; and they shall walk, and not faint. (Isaiah 40:31 KJV)

It was timely because I knew the journey that was ahead of me required strength, strength that I didn't have at the time. It was a struggle to get my rhythm back. It seemed as though I was a step behind every play. It was frustrating, but like I said before, basketball is seventy percent mental; and once my mind caught up, my body did the same.

Everyone counted us out that year. At one point, we lost five games in a row. Losing games like that was foreign to me, but we eventually got back on track, and regardless of the outsiders doubting us, we still held on to the belief that we had what it took to bring another state championship back to Tucker. As the playoffs began, we needed to win five games to make that happen, but we would only win four.

We fell to Miller Grove in the state finals. It was set up for us just like it was in 2007. Back then we had lost to rival Columbia a couple times during the regular season before beating them in the finals. And now we had lost to Miller Grove a couple times during the regular season before facing them in the finals. One could only think that it was our destiny to win it all, but there wouldn't be a story book ending for us, and we would lose by a wide margin. Even though the game was out of reach, something deep within was telling me to "keep playing hard." So, I played like we were down by one until Coach Hartry took me out in the last few minutes of the game.

It was hard watching someone hoist up a trophy that we felt should have been ours. It was almost like seeing your girl with another guy. But we came in thinking that they were just going to hand us the game because we were Tucker, and it didn't happen like that. Unfortunately, losses are a part of the game.

About a week later, I received a letter in the mail. It was from Kennesaw State University, which was a division one school about forty minutes from Tucker. I opened it up to find a hand written letter:

Brandon,

It was a pleasure watching you in the playoffs and the state championship game. I thought it was remarkable how you continued to play hard even when the game was out of reach. We want you to come to our camp that we'll be hosting this summer. Give me a call when you get a chance.

- Coach Matta

Coach Matta was the head assistant coach at Kennesaw State. We played there during the brutal summer going into my sophomore year. They had a beautiful campus and nice facilities. The initial call between Coach Matta and I was brief, but I could tell that he was passionate about what he was doing. He informed me that they had me on their radar for a while and invited me to the camp they would be hosting for recruits that summer. At the time, I didn't know much about Kennesaw, nor did I know of any other schools that were seriously interested in me, but it seemed like they were looking to give me an opportunity. So, I told him to send me the information and that I would be there.

When I got to camp, I noticed that there were a lot of guys who were from Georgia there. There were even a few guys there who we knocked off during our state playoff run that year. The camp consisted of drills, a tour of campus, and scrimmage games to end the day. Coach Tony Ingle, who was Kennesaw's head coach, sat us all down and spoke to us around lunch time. He said something that I've never forgotten, "the most important decisions you'll ever make in your life, are where you go to school, and who you're going to marry." I didn't know it at the time, but Coach was right. Those aren't decisions like choosing what to wear or eat. Those were life altering decisions, meaning they had the power to somewhat determine the direction in which your life was headed; And although marriage was something that wouldn't be happening for a while, my decision as to which school I would attend wasn't that far away.

When camp was finished, Coach Matta walked me to my car. "All the coaches were impressed with what they saw out there from you today. We'll be in touch soon", he said as he smiled and shook my hand. I got in my car and didn't know what to think. I felt I played well that day, but "we'll be in touch soon" was usually code for "don't expect us to call." Regardless of whether they called me or not, I knew that I was taking steps in the right direction, and I could feel myself mounting up just as an eagle mounts up toward the sky. I found satisfaction in that.

Vision
"Where there is no vision, the people perish..."
(Proverbs 29:18 KJV)

The summer going into my senior year the AAU team that I had played with since I was twelve years old had broken up. We had quite a few two sport athletes and lots of them had realized that football was the route they wanted to take. It felt like our family had been torn apart, but I saw it coming. The year before when we got back from our last tournament in Las Vegas, NV, I watched everyone grab their luggage from baggage claim and make their way to their parents who had come to pick them up. I was the last one to leave; And as I watched everyone gather their belongings, I knew that would be the last time we would play together. I got the same feeling that I felt when I watched the last episode of Martin, The Fresh Prince, or Living Single. I knew that we had a great run, but I also knew that it was over.

So, I didn't play with The Atlanta Select that year, I was now playing with the Georgia Stars, who had been one of our rivals since I started playing AAU basketball. Greg Smarr, we just called him Coach Greg, was our coach, and our team was comprised mostly of the North Clayton High School basketball team. North Clayton was a school on the southside of town, not too far from the airport. We actually practiced at North Clayton so I would drive out there from Tucker twice a week. I had been playing against these guys for years, and we went at it on the court. Our games were always filled with trash talking, high intensity, and physical play; but I always had respect for them, and from the first practice they welcomed me with open arms. I didn't know much about Coach Greg, but from years of playing against him I knew he was fiery. He was always up on the sidelines yelling during games. But from day one, he let me know that he was excited to have me and really believed in my game. He encouraged me to do things on the court like more ball handling and putting me in more playmaking situations. He didn't put any restrictions on us as players and let us play our game while allowing us to grow through our mistakes. Most of the coaches that I had up to that point had a style similar to that, but I wouldn't learn to appreciate it until a few years later.

The summer was coming to a close, and it was time for the AAU Nationals to start. The Nationals was a tournament usually held in Orlando, FL at the Disney Sports Complex where the best teams from all over the country would come together and compete for the #1 spot. I had played in the Nationals before, and it was no joke. It was one week of straight basketball. This is the place where you make a name for yourself. This was also my last tournament. In fact, it was all of our last tournaments. We had reached the seventeen year old age limit and this was essentially our last opportunity to impress college coaches before our high school senior seasons began. There were lots of schools that had shown interest in me, but no one had actually put an offer on the table, not even Kennesaw State.

I was carrying my bags to my dad's truck on the morning I was set to leave. My dad was going to drop me off with Coach Greg and I'd ride down with him and the rest of the team. My mom stopped me as I was coming through the kitchen. "Honey, this is your last chance. You go down there and do what you need to do!" she said. Then we prayed,

I gave her a kiss, and I left.

I knew that I had the skills to play collegiately, what worried me was the time that it was taking for someone to make an offer. Coaches had been calling for months and coming to my school to see me, but it seemed like everyone was afraid to pull the trigger. "We're really interested in you" seemed to be the phrase that all the coaches used. I was tired of hearing that, it felt like torture. I was growing anxious, and I knew my time was coming; I just didn't know when. Strangely enough though, when I prayed with my mom in the kitchen that day, I felt a peace that I hadn't felt in a long time. Instantly, I just knew that everything was going to be alright. I didn't know how things were going to work out, but I just knew they would, I could feel it the entire ride down to Orlando. I went down there with zero scholarship offers, but I came back with six.

Florida Gulf Coast University, Bethune-Cookman, Florida A&M, Tennessee Tech, USC Upstate, and Kennesaw State University. That was six opportunities to go to college for free and pursue not only a higher education, but my dream of playing professional basketball. There were six groups of coaches who thought that I was worth it and decided to take a chance on me. I thought that was awesome. From the time I was about twelve years old, my dad would tell me about this window of opportunity. He would say the window was wide open, but the older I got, the smaller the window would become. I noticed that with basketball. At that time, there were three hundred fifty division one schools in the NCAA. Each one of those schools had thirteen scholarships per year. That's a total of 4,550 players that could compete at that level per year. That might seem like a lot of positions but when you factor in the number of high school players competing for those spots on a yearly basis, you'd see that it's not. I was now blessed with the opportunity to be one of those fortunate few. I remember some of my "friends" and teammates at the time joking that my dad would probably be making the decision as to where I would be going to school because he was such a heavy influence in my life. To be honest, it hurt me. I thought they would be happy for me because they knew the amount of work I put in for this. Instead, they were jealous and tried to disguise their envy as a "joke." It opened my eyes to something that my parents had always told me but I could never grasp, "Everyone you hang around ain't your friend."

That list of six schools had grown to about twelve in just a couple months, and other schools had begun to show interest as well. It was like the floodgates had been opened. By this time, my senior season had started and every night coaches were calling. My Dad would take me and a legal pad in the living room to talk to these coaches for what seemed like hours. I grew frustrated. I didn't want to spend every night of my senior year talking to coaches. I didn't want to have to play the entire season and worry about where I was going to school. I was tired of hearing the same questions and answers every night. I just wanted to be free.

One night, we had finished talking to a coach from the west coast around 11pm our time, so around 8pm his time. I was exhausted, and I was fed up with talking to coaches. This decision was becoming a burden. I weighed the pros and cons of every school that offered me a scholarship, and honestly, I didn't know who to choose; But I knew I couldn't go on like this. I glanced at the clock as I lied in bed. It was 11:45pm and I decided to pray one of the simplest prayers that

I've ever prayed. "Lord, show me where to go to school." Exactly fifteen minutes later, I heard something outside. I got out of bed and made my way to the window. I opened it, and I heard an owl. "Hoot Hoo! Hoot Hoo!" I couldn't see it, but I heard it loud and clear, and I knew God was speaking to me. That was my sign. Kennesaw State Owls. The next day I called Coach Matta and set up my official visit.

An official visit was when the school would bring you out to visit their school for a couple days. They would pay for your travel, your lodging, your food, and entertainment. NCAA regualtions gave you a maximum of five college visits during the recruiting process, and I had already taken two. My first visit was to Florida Gulf Coast University (FGCU), who played in the same conference as Kennesaw. They were located in Fort Meyers, FL, which wasn't too far from Miami. I went down there with my parents and one of my high school teammates. It was beautiful, and I Loved their arena, but I wasn't sold. I knew better than to jump at the first opportunity that was thrown my way.

My next visit was to the illustrious Bethune-Cookman University, an HBCU in Daytona Beach, FL. You're probably thinking, "why is he visiting all these Florida schools?" Basically, I wanted to be somewhere warm, and I always seemed to play well in Florida. It was as if the Florida sun drew the best out of me. My dad made the trip down to Bethune with me, which was scheduled during their homecoming. Lots of schools liked to bring in recruits around events like homecoming to draw you in, but it never gives a true representation of the atmosphere. On official visits, they usually give one of the players the responsibility of being your host. This means you show the recruit around, take them to some parties, and really let them experience campus life. My host was Aric Miller. We played together my first two years of high school. Aric was about 6'4 and had a great feel for the game. To me, he played a lot like Deron Williams. After college, he had a great deal of success playing in the Australian professional leagues.

Overall, I was really feelin' Bethune, until we got to the living arrangements; And that's where they lost me. At FGCU the players lived in apartment style dorms, meaning everyone had their own room, and privacy. At Bethune, you shared a room with your teammate and in a few instances, you could be living with someone who wasn't your teammate. The worst part about it was that you weren't allowed to have the opposite sex in your room. "Yo Aric, so where do you take girls if you want to spend some time with them?" I asked. "You just gotta find another spot…or take em to the gym", he replied. That was a deal breaker for me. I had been sneaking girls in and out of my parents' house for the past few years, I couldn't spend my college years doing the same. Also, they played in an older, smaller facility that felt like a high school gym. To be honest, my middle school gym might've been bigger. I was going to college, and I wanted it to feel like I was playing in college, not high school. On the way back to Atlanta my Dad asked, "so what do you think?" "I don't think that's the school for me, I wanna keep my options open." I replied. "It was the dorms that did it huh?" He said as he laughed. "Yep."

My Dad and I both liked Kennesaw State, but there was one problem…it was too close. We would go up there on Sundays and I would scrimmage against their players and some of the other guys they were recruiting. I had even started to develop a relationship with some of the players and I felt like I was at home whenever I was there. My Dad wanted me to go somewhere further away so I'd be able to gain more life experience and I still had Florida on my mind; But after God had given me that sign, I knew that I had to at least give Kennesaw an opportunity.

Since Kennesaw was only about thirty miles away, I drove up on a chilly Saturday morning in November. I arrived around eight o'clock, just in time to catch their morning practice. I sat on the sidelines in their practice facility intently watching them go through drills and paying close attention to detail. I saw how Coach Ingle and his staff interacted with the players and corrected them when mistakes were made. Coach Ingle had been doing this for a long time, and his wisdom and knowledge of the game were on display. I also took notice of their practice facility. It was nicer than the gym that Bethune played their actual games in.

When practice was over, Coach Matta hooked me up with my host, Markeith Cummings. Markeith was one of the players I had started to build a relationship with when I came up to play on Sundays. He was about 6'6, strong, and could jump out of the gym. Him and I also had very similar skill sets. We both were able to play inside and on the perimeter. Even some of our movements on the court were alike. In that practice, I took note of where they played Markeith and realized that I could be in the same positions.

Markeith and I went to eat at the cafeteria when we left the practice facility. Kennesaw had just upgraded their dining hall and was considered to have one of the best cafeterias in the country; and this was unlike any cafeteria I had seen before. They had stations where you could get different types of food. They had an American station where you could get hot dogs and cheeseburgers, an Asian station, an Italian station, a salad bar, and a dessert station. You could get just about anything that you wanted in there. While we ate, I asked Markeith all kinds of questions about the coaches, the team, and the campus life, and he kept it real with me by telling me the good and the bad.

Coach Matta came and picked me up when we left the cafeteria and took me around campus and the city of Kennesaw. Later that night, I got back up with Markeith and we hit a couple hang out spots. We went back to his apartment to try and find another move for the night, but I had seen enough and was ready to get back to the hotel and go to sleep. As I was sitting in the living room, I noticed that everyone there had their own room, and I had just one question left. "Yo man, quick question. Can you have girls in your apartment here?" He looked at me like I was crazy and replied, "Yeah man, we grown here." I laughed and let him know that one of the schools I visited made you share a room, and you couldn't have girls in there. He told me that would have been a deal breaker for him too. Markeith dropped me off at the hotel afterwards.

The next day Coach Matta came and got me for breakfast. Then he took me to Kennesaw Mountain, which was the location of The Battle of Kennesaw Mountain during the Civil War. We stood at the summit and were able to see out for miles. We could see all the way to Stone Mountain, which was on my side of town. Coach told me this was the place that he came to think and clear his head. I could see why, it was beautiful up there.

Later that day my parents made the forty-five-minute drive to

Kennesaw that afternoon to meet with the coaching staff. Coach Matta, Coach Ingle, Coach Robinson, Coach Roth, my parents and myself all sat down in Coach Ingle's office to discuss my visit and my possible future at Kennesaw State University. Coach had a table in his office that was an exact replica of the court they played on. He began to talk about his vision for the program, and his vision for me. The more he talked, the more excited he got. Spit started to fly as he broke out in a sweat and his southern accent reached its' highest decibel. Then, he banged on the replica table right near the free throw line and yelled "It makes no sense that the University of Georgia has never won a basketball national championship on any level, and they were the first chartered state university in Georgia." Coach had won a division two national championship just five years before in 2004, and now that Kennesaw was a division one school and eligible for the NCAA tournament, he was looking to win another. His passion was drawing me closer, and as I listened to him speak, the wheels were turning in my mind. I wanted to play for someone like Coach Ingle. He believed in me, and he had vision.

He finished speaking and his face changed from red back to white and he asked me, "now Brandon, what do you want to do?" All eyes were on me. Without any doubt in my mind, I said "I wanna play here." I knew Kennesaw was the right place for me, and I think if I would have chosen another school, I would have seriously regretted it. Two weeks later I signed my National Letter of Intent in the library at my school in front of my family, friends, and coaches. I was officially a Kennesaw State Owl.

Hearing Coach Ingle speak about his vision for the program with the coaches and my parents that day was monumental. He was a dreamer, much like myself, and he didn't care about the obstacles that were before him. I realized that vision wasn't just having a dream, vision was being able to see the steps to achieve that dream, even when others couldn't. See, I had a dream, but what I needed to develop was my vision.

Flipping Tables

"Jesus entered the Temple and began to drive out the people buying and selling animals for sacrifices. He knocked over the tables of the money changers and the chairs of those selling doves, and He stopped everyone from using the Temple as a marketplace."
(Mark 11:15-16 NLT)

Mark 11:15-16 is one of my favorite portions of scripture because it shows just how gangsta Jesus was and is. I used to think Jesus was this quiet guy who walked around with his arms folded, and constantly saying things like, "Peace be unto you." But Jesus was a rebel. He wasn't afraid to go against the grain. He wasn't afraid to challenge the regime. He wasn't afraid to flip a table or two.

I signed my scholarship, and the daunting recruiting process was now over. I could play my senior season in peace, just as I intended, but peace has a price. One thing I've learned is that being a "nice" guy will have you sitting back and watching someone else live your dream. People try to take advantage of those who are nice, soft spoken, or calm because they think they aren't able to stand up for themselves. They expect those people to just sit back and accept whatever comes their way; And they might do that for a while, but there's only so much that a person can take before they reach their limit.

Coach Matta said to me one day, "I know the kinda guy you are." "What do you mean?" I asked. "You're a quiet guy, but you're not quiet because you're weak. You're quiet because you're strong. The guy that comes in the bar loud and yelling isn't the guy you have to worry about, it's the guy sitting in the back by himself and not saying anything. He's the one you have to watch, he's the one that will kill you." Even though I was a good basketball player, I realized that I still had to fight for my respect. Being good at basketball only got me respect on the court, I needed it in everyday life as well. I was kind, quiet, and I wasn't the type of person who was known for causing a commotion; And lots of people saw that as a weakness.

After my junior season, lots of the players that helped get us to the state finals had graduated and moved on. My senior year, we had a few talented guys come in from neighboring schools. Personality wise, they fit right in, but they all seemed to have their own agendas. They were more focused on individual success as opposed to us succeeding as a team. They didn't realize that the further we went as a team, the more recognition they would receive as individuals from scouts and college coaches. As I got older, I started to see this pattern of thinking within the black community. We were always in competition with one another while other races were able to come together and uplift themselves.

We were about four games into the season, and so far, we had struggled with every team that we played against; Even though we were better than all of them. We played on a Saturday night at home, and I was having a rough game. I was frustrated because I was barely touching the ball. I attempted five shots in two games, and it was almost as if the plan was to not pass the ball to me.

Coach Hartry pulled me out and I sat on the end of the bench. I took off my shooting sleeve and threw it on the baseline near our cheerleaders. "Pick it up!" I heard my dad yell from the first row on the opposite side of the court. I sat there ignoring him and disgusted by our play that night. "Pick it up!" he yelled again, this time with a little more bass in his voice. Although I was mad, I knew if I didn't pick up that shooting sleeve, I would have some problems when I got home. I made my way to the baseline and picked up the sleeve. We ended up winning but everyone in the gym knew there was something wrong with me.

When we got to the locker room Coach begins to talk about how horribly we played that night. Then he switched gears and said, "Dawson, I don't know who is in your ear, but you ain't did nothing since you signed those bull**** a** scholarship papers!" Coach Hartry was never one to hold his tongue and I respected him for that, but now wasn't the time to admire the man he was, now was the time to flip a table. I learned early on to pick your battles. Sometimes you have to handle a situation head on and sometimes you have to walk away; But this wasn't the time to walk away. Sometimes you only get one opportunity to impact a situation and I knew if I didn't say anything at that moment, things would never change. I stood up, smirked, and let out an arrogant chuckle. "In my ear?" I asked. "There's no one in my ear. The problem is you let these nig*** come over here and just play however they wanna play. That's bull**** and you know it!" The locker room was so silent that you could hear an ant whisper and Coach looked at me, shocked that I would even challenge him like that. What I realized was that this wasn't just about basketball, it was about respect. They weren't passing me the ball because they felt that I would just accept it and go with the flow because I was a "nice guy", but I refused to flow with that current. I knew I could've gotten kicked off the team for talking to Coach that way, but I valued my respect far more than I valued my place on that team. For a long time, I thought that Christian people had to be quiet, subdued, and nice which is sometimes why I chose not to say things that I felt should be said in certain situations. It wasn't until years later when I read about Jesus going into the temple and flipping up tables did I learn that sometimes you have to cause a ruckus in order to get your point across. Sometimes you have to let people know that you're not a punk and be willing to stand up for what you believe in regardless of the consequences.

Monday came around and I proceeded with life as I normally would. I hadn't talked with any of my coaches, and I didn't know if I was still a part of the team. To be honest, I had never had an outburst toward any of my coaches like that, but from seeing other people do it, things never ended well.

I was sitting in my first period class when I heard a knock at the door. It was Coach Lamar. He asked my teacher if he could speak with me. I walked out of the classroom prepared to hear the consequences I would have to face or how disappointed the coaching staff was with me. "How you feelin man?" he asked. "I'm all good Coach." That was usually my reply whenever someone asked how I was doing even if things weren't "all good." "Look man, I know you're frustrated, and we've noticed what the problem is, and we're gonna correct it. But you're the leader of this team. These guys are gonna follow you. So, if they see you getting frustrated and falling apart, they're gonna do the same." Coach was right. I couldn't allow my emotions to dictate my actions, no matter how frustrated I was with the situation. We dapped each other up, and I went back to class.

Almost the second I got back to class, I got a call to come to the principal's office. Boy was I popular this morning. Mr. Jackson, or Coach Jackson as we all called him was our principal. He was a football coach at one point, hence the reason we called him coach. He was about 6'2, two hundred fifty pounds of muscle, stern, and he did not play. He was quick to correct you when you were out of line, and he didn't care who you were either. One time he took my skully because I was wearing it in the building. Star basketball player or not, no one was above the law in his hallways. I never saw that skully ever again either.

I walked into his office, rifling through my mind what I could have possibly done that would have warranted a trip to the principal's office. My best guess was that they saw me on the security cameras skipping first period or something. "Dawson, have a seat man", he said to me as I shut the door behind me. "At the game on Saturday, I saw you take your sleeve off and throw it when you came out of the game. I know you're frustrated, but you've already signed your scholarship. Let some of these other guys shine." Now, this is what I was talking about when I said people would try to take advantage of those who were considered "nice" or came off as a calm individual like myself. He was suggesting that I be Robin and allow someone else to be Batman. Let's be clear, if there was someone else there who was better than me and capable of being Batman, I would have put on the Robin costume; but on that team I knew my role. I was Batman.

I don't think I said anything. All I could do was shake my head in disbelief, as I walked out of his office. I couldn't understand why everyone thought that I should take a backseat just so someone else could shine. Coach Jackson was a former athlete himself. He knew that wasn't how the game was played.

I stepped into the hallway and called my dad. "Dad, Coach Jackson just called me into his office and told me since I already had a scholarship, to let some of these other guys on the team shine." If you've ever met my dad, then you know that he doesn't know what second place is. My dad was athlete of the year at his high school; He played basketball, football, baseball, and ran track. He went to Alabama State on a baseball and football scholarship and had a shot at playing pro baseball before he hurt his shoulder. He would always say to my brothers and I, "I set the bar high", and to be honest, he did. When I told him what happened all I heard was "Ok." But it wasn't an "Ok, that's fine." It was an "Ok, I'll handle this."

After school, I went to practice as I normally would. I expected Coach Hartry to say something about Saturday night to me in front of the team. Instead, he came into the gym skipping, filled with energy, high fiving anyone in his vicinity. "Let's go baby!" was all you heard throughout the gym. He came to me, dapped me up, and embraced me. Then looked me in the eyes and said, "Let's get after it today!" Translation, "I know how you're feeling, I understand. Thank you for bringing it to my attention. Now, let's get to work." But since I had made those statements, that meant that I had to back up my claims. I had to elevate my game. I had to produce.

When I got home that night, I found my parents talking in the kitchen. My dad had that serious face on, but my mom was laughing. I could tell that my dad had just told a story, and my mom found it hilarious. "What's up?" I asked. "Your dad was just telling me what he told the principal when he called the school today", My mom said. "Y-You called the school?" I asked as my eyes almost popped out of my head. I found out their conversation went something like this:

Dad: "Principal Jackson, You've got a son, right?"
Principal Jackson: "Yes"
Dad: "And would you ever tell him to be 2nd place?"
Principal Jackson: "No, I wouldn't"
Dad: "Alright then, don't ever tell my son to be 2nd place."

My Dad and I haven't always seen eye to eye. I know he Loved me, but I thought at times he pushed me a bit too hard. I remember after my middle school games I would come home and eat, then I'd have a shower, maybe watch television for a second, and finally get in bed around 11pm. Thirty minutes later he would come in my room and hook his camera up to my VCR. "Get up, we gotta watch this game from tonight." For the next hour and a half, I would be fighting to keep my eyes open as my Dad highlighted the mistakes I made or areas where I could have been better from that night's game.

I didn't understand why we had to watch the game that same night. I thought I would have been just fine waiting until the next day to watch it, but my dad knew that if we delayed, it would probably never get done. Watching film helped me recognize situations on the court quicker and keep me from making the same mistakes. Even games where I felt I had minimal mistakes, the camera (and my dad) proved otherwise. It didn't matter if I had twenty points or two, "you could always be better somewhere" my dad would say. Some people might say that's a bit overboard and obsessive, but my dad was operating out of a wisdom that was far too advanced for me to grasp. He understood that the quicker I realized those mistakes, the quicker I could hone in on them. He was also letting me know that there were still a lot of holes in my game, a means by which he kept me humble.

Later that season we played against Marist in the region tournament. All we had to do was win that game and we'd be heading back to the playoffs. Coach Hartry had told us the night before that if we won, he would be making his eighth consecutive state playoff appearance which would have set a new record in DeKalb County. I wanted that record for him, but we found ourselves down by three against Marist with two seconds left on the clock. We called a timeout and Coach Lamar says, "We got two seconds left, who wants the last shot!" Marist was a private school that was bigger than some colleges. The gym was packed, people were screaming, and you could cut the tension in there with a knife. I could feel the uneasy energy coming from my teammates. This was my team, my senior year, and I had scored our last eight points. I didn't want to leave it up to anyone but myself. I was Batman.

Before anyone could answer I said with a boldness that was somewhat foreign to me, "I WANT IT COACH!" He proceeds to draw up the play on the whiteboard that we're all gathered around. The buzzer sounds signaling that the timeout is over and it's time to get back on the floor. We all line up in our spots, and the referee hands my teammate the ball to inbound. I was supposed to come off the screen and take the shot, but there was one problem…the screen never came. Everyone panicked and did something completely contrary to what Coach had drawn up.

The play is blown.

I find a way to get open.

I get the ball.

I jab right.

I go left.

Elevate.

And shoot.

This was the moment that all players dream of. This was the shot that I practiced in my driveway as a kid, counting down, imagining that this was to win the NBA finals. This was a shot that I've made a thousand times throughout my career, whether it be in games, practice, or workouts. But not this time. The shot was on-line, but the ball ricocheted off the back rim as time expired. I stood at center court in disbelief as the crowd rushed the floor. Tears begin to run down my face as members of the opposing team come up and congratulate me on my performance. My dad and Josh found me in the sea of people. Dad embraces me and lets me know that he's proud of me. Although I'm hurt that I'll never put on that tucker uniform again and frustrated because I know this season shouldn't have ended like that, my tears don't last long. We might have lost the game, but I had found something that night. I was searching for myself, and up to that point I felt like I was being who everyone else wanted and needed me to be, but not who I wanted and needed myself to be. But that night, I got a glimpse of something within me that I always knew was there but wasn't able to pull it out on a consistent basis.

The Bible says, "to be as bold as a lion" (Prov. 28:1). I had heard that verse all my life, but I didn't consider myself to be bold. When

I thought of bold, my parents came to mind. Neither of them were ever afraid to say what needed to be said, when it needed to be said. But I didn't have that. I was afraid to say certain things to people that needed to be said which was to my detriment because I knew the power of my words. In my own life I observed how physical wounds from playing basketball or getting into fights would often heal quickly; but harsh words from people lasted for what seemed like forever. This meant the old adage "sticks and stones may break my bones, but words will never hurt me", was a complete lie. Yet that night when Coach drew up the play in the huddle and asked, "who wants the last shot?" the same boldness that had come over me in the locker room earlier that season, arose in me once again. In the back of my mind, I knew that if I missed, people would talk about me, but I didn't care. In that moment, I wasn't worried about what other people thought about me. In that moment there was no doubt. In that moment, I wasn't afraid.

Friends

"There are "friends" who destroy each other, but a real friend sticks closer than a brother."
(Proverbs 18:24 NLT)

I had spent my entire summer playing basketball, but that's all that I was doing "playing". I was competing against other collegiate players, but I wasn't working on anything. I didn't add to my game like I had done in years past. A big part of me felt as though I had wasted that summer, another part of me was excited for this new chapter in my life. I didn't really know what to expect from college. All of my mentors gave me different perspectives and things to be mindful of as I entered this next part of my journey. My dad said that it would be "the best four years of my life." Rahn told me that it would be "crazy", but he also advised me to stay focused above all. But that wasn't enough for me. I knew that I would have fun, but I needed more details. Details specifically about Kennesaw.

When I was in the tenth grade, I had a technology teacher named Mrs. Stephens. Her husband was the new head football coach. They had moved from Camden County Georgia, and both taken positions at Tucker. Mrs. Stephens had been in the military, so she was strict and disciplined. I would come down the stairs and see her standing at attention with her hands behind her back outside of her classroom. If the bell rung and you didn't make it in on time, you were late, and you'd be locked out. No exceptions. I liked to joke and play around, and occasionally that caused me to be a couple minutes late to some of my other classes, but I knew she didn't play; so I made sure I was in there before the door closed. But even though Mrs. Stephens was the no-nonsense type, she was extra cool. We would laugh and joke all the time, well, once I got my work done.

One day an older girl came in and sat with Mrs. Stephens. She was wearing a visitors badge so I knew she wasn't enrolled at Tucker. Me being the naturally inquisitive person I am, decided to go over to Mrs. Stephens desk and investigate a bit further. "Brandon, meet Tia", Mrs. Stephens said. At first, I figured that Tia was Mrs. Stephens daughter, but I would later find out that she was a friend of the family and had moved to Atlanta with Mr. and Mrs. Stephens. Tia would visit our class often, and every time I saw her, we would strike up a conversation. I didn't know Tia at all, but she was one of those people that had an inviting spirit. She always had on a smile, and she always made you feel welcome, regardless of whether she knew you or not. She was one of the coolest people that I would ever meet. Over the next two years, it felt like I saw her just about every time she came up to visit Mrs. Stephens.

When my senior year came around and Mrs. Stephens found out that I was going to Kennesaw, she said "you know that's where Tia goes! I'm gonna pass her number to you. Call her, I'm sure she'll tell you everything you need to know about Kennesaw." As I was leaving the gym one day after a workout, I decided to give Tia a call. We probably talked for an hour, and Tia gave me the complete run-down about the school; Things to look out for as a freshman, places to go, places to not go, things to do on campus, etc. I always felt that genuine people were hard to come by, but after our conversation, I knew that Tia was the real deal. Up to that point in my life, I didn't have many people that I trusted outside of my family and my mentors. I learned first-hand that people will turn on you, and not everyone you meet can be trusted; Also, the fact that Adrian and I were in a somewhat long-distance relationship at the time didn't help my trust issues either. I was extremely cautious, and suspicious of everyone I came across. In my mind, allowing people to get close to you and see who you truly were, was just a way of empowering them to hurt you.

Things were different with Tia though. I had no reservations about her, and I got a sense that we were in similar places. Both of us were embarking on new journeys, stepping outside of what was comfortable to us and venturing into the unknown. I trusted her and I felt that she trusted me too.

I believe that every friendship has a defining moment, a situation that would set the tone for the relationship. For Tia and I, that moment would come when she asked me to help her and her best friend, Tangie, movie into their new apartment. They had this brown couch, which we got up the stairs and into the apartment pretty easy. The hard part came when I had to put the legs on it. Three of the four legs went on smoothly, but I couldn't find the grooves to fit the last leg on. I struggled with it for about ten minutes. Finally, I rigged it up and hoped that it would stay. Then once we were finished moving all the boxes in, I left. I came back the next day and the first question I asked when I walked in was, "So, how's the couch?" They both laughed hysterically and said, "Boy! You know you didn't put those legs on that couch right!"

We had a good laugh about that, but that moment helped set the tone for our relationship. Tia and Tangie became like big sisters to me, and I was their little brother. They looked out for me and always showed Love. My freshman year, my apartment was about five minutes from theirs, so I would have dinner at their place almost every week, which was extremely clutch for a broke college student-athlete. One of the best aspects of our relationship was the communication. We would talk for hours at the dinner table (and on that brown couch) about life, dreams, ideas, our fears, and our hopes. I was able to tell them things I couldn't tell anyone else. I trusted them, and they trusted me, well, not when it came to assembling furniture.

August 10th, 2010, was move in day at Kennesaw, a day that I had waited for for quite some time. I looked forward to the freedom. I thought I was grown anyway, and now was my chance to prove it. I Loved my parents, but it was time for me to step out from under their wings and begin to spread my own.

My room was packed up and boxes were all over the floor. Everything that had any sentimental value was packed into those boxes; I even made sure that I had the blanket my Aunty Dot made for me when I was a kid, the one with the basketball patch. Most people wouldn't bring a baby blanket to college, but I wasn't most people; Plus, I hoped it would continue to serve as a reminder and keep me focused. With the boxes covering the floor, I had to create a pathway so I could get to and from my bed. My dad had been yelling at me for the past week, and I was confused about why he was getting mad at me for every little thing. I was frustrated and counting down the days until I left. Seeing my frustration, my mom came and gave me some insight as to what was going on. She was always good for giving me wisdom when I really needed it. "He's upset because he's going to miss you" she said. My dad and I were super close. He would always say, he was my biggest fan and my biggest critic, and he still is to this day.

My dad was old school, and was as tough as they come. He was the type to pack a wound with dirt and keep on moving. I remember having an AAU game one Sunday morning, and if you've played AAU, you know how important the Sunday games are. I think we were scheduled to play across town at 8:30am or something ridiculously early like that. I was up at 6am, waiting for him to come in the room and tell me to get ready, but then it was 6:10, and 6:30, and my dad still hadn't come out of my parents room. At 6:45 I get up and go in there. He's in bed groaning in pain. "Yo dad, you getting up?" I asked. "Yeah man, just give me a second."

I go back in my room and start to get ready. He walks out at 7 holding his side. "Come on, let's go." I didn't know what was going on, but I could tell that he was in pain. I wouldn't find out until later that day that he had kidney stones, but if he didn't tell you, you wouldn't know it. He coached and yelled like nothing was wrong through all three of the games we played that day.

I was fourteen, but that was the was the day I learned what true toughness was. Being tough wasn't punching somebody in the face because they said something you didn't like, nah, that's actually pretty weak. Someone who is truly tough can endure, and keep going when conditions aren't favorable.

My dad had physical toughness but expressing how he felt was something that he still needed to work on. He was from an era where you were deemed as weak if you were a man and expressed your feelings. Before I went to college, I think I had only heard him say "I Love you" to my brothers and I maybe five times or so in my life.

The first time I truly remember was when I was in the eighth grade and one his best friends son's was shot and killed. He had known him since he was a baby, and his life was cut short in his twenties. I remember him calling us into the living room and wrapping his arms around us and saying, "I Love yall." He said it with great sorrow in his voice. It was a heavy moment, and it was weird to me because I rarely saw that side of him. I wasn't the type that needed to be told "I Love you" all the time either. I knew he and my mom Loved us, although my mom was far more prone to saying it. After my mom enlightened me on what was going on with my dad, my perspective changed, and I did my best to enjoy the last few days we had together.

When move-in day came, I was up before the sun putting boxes in my dad's truck. The same truck that I used to hate to see pull up to the school when I knew that I was in trouble, would now be the chariot that would whisk me away to a land of freedom and endless possibility.

I had still considered myself to be a bit of a lone wolf, suspicious of everyone who attempted to come into my life. I was never the standoffish type. I could play the game and make you feel welcomed, but you'd better believe I was watching you like a hawk. The gates that I had erected around myself were so high that not even LeBron James could jump them. But sometimes, The Lord just gives people a key to the gates allowing them access into the innermost parts of you. Tia was one of those people, and Nick Turner would be the next.

There were four players moving in that day. We all stood on a hill where one of the apartments were located and waited for instructions from our team manager on what to do next. "Ok fellas, welcome to Kennesaw. Go down this hill to the table and give them your name and pick up your keys." Said Jeff, our team manager. I turned and began to walk down the hill with my eyes locked onto table that held the keys to opening the next door of my journey. As I'm walking down the hill, I glance to my right and see a dude two inches from my face. "Hey, I'm Nick!" he said. I leaned back with a look on my face that said, "Yo, back up man!" "What's good man, I'm Brandon." I would later find out that Nick had tripped as we were going down the hill which caused him to be all in my grill during our first interaction.

Instantly this guy began to talk to me like we had known each other. I met his mom a few minutes later after we picked up our keys, and she talked to me like she knew me as well. It was the weirdest thing and also extremely refreshing. As my dad and I moved my stuff in, I kept trying to figure out where I knew them from, but I didn't. I had never seen them in my life. It was funny though; I'd been around them for all of ten minutes and I was comfortable with them; That was something I wasn't accustomed to feeling.

Nick was from Indianapolis, IN, and he was all about basketball. This man Loved the game and was dang near a historian of it. He could tell you about any player that has ever played in the NBA, and he knew about all the top prospects coming in. He was basically a basketball encyclopedia. But on top of all this knowledge he had about the game, he was equally as knowledgeable about things of the world. He knew different musicians, artists, historical facts, and random trivia. He was probably the most well-rounded person I had ever met. Oh, and not to mention he had tight handles and a silky jump shot.

Over the next few years, Nick wouldn't only become one of my best friends, but my brother. We grew together, pushed each other on the court, and challenged one another off of it. Nick was one of those brutally honest people that I had grown to Love. What I admired most about Nick was the fact that he never lied to me. He was able to tell me the truth when it was easy, and when it was hard. That's how he gained my respect.

My Dad and I finished moving my things in and we got ready to say our goodbyes. We walked down to his truck, he handed me a box of condoms and said, "Don't make no babies, and don't call me and your momma every day. You only call on Sundays." Then he drove off. The funny part about that is, he's called me just about every day for the past twelve years.

Identity

"For there is nothing covered, that shall not be revealed; neither hid, that shall not be known."

(Luke 12:2 KJV)

Coming in as a freshman I felt as though I had to make a name for myself on and off the court. I was in a new environment with new people, and I felt like this was an opportunity to create my own narrative. For so long I felt like I was wearing a mask, and no one knew the real me. I wore that mask so much that I barely knew myself. I had an idea of who I was, but my true identity still remained a mystery.

During my senior year of high school, I picked up the nickname, "Breeze." It just kind of came out of nowhere, and at first I wasn't a fan of it; But the more I heard it, the more I started to like it. It stuck, and it followed me from Tucker to Kennesaw. People honestly thought it was my real name, even my coaches called me Breeze. I thought it was cool, but deep down, I knew it was just another mask; Another coping mechanism that would prevent me from putting in the work to find out who I truly was.

Off the court, the things that I did in secret in high school, I could now do openly. I was smoking, drinking, and having sex with different women just about every night. My hope was that through these channels of what I thought was "manhood" I would come to this divine revelation of who I truly was; Instead, these things lead me further into confusion about my identity. By not having a true grasp of manhood or identity, you can find yourself in some situations that can not only jeopardize your life, but your freedom as well.

One night, Drew and I went to a small party on campus. We were leaving early the next morning to go play Alabama State, so we didn't plan on being there long, we just wanted to get out for a bit. When we got there, a young lady comes up to us and says, "I Love black guys!" We can tell she's been drinking, but we just laugh, pour ourselves a drink, and begin to enjoy the atmosphere. As the night goes on, she continues to flirt with us, primarily me. She's touching my leg and doing her best to get me to come into her room with her. I'm reluctant at first, but then I lean over to Drew and say, "Yo, this chick wanna have sex. I'm gonna step off in the room right quick." There's only about ten people in the apartment, all of them being her friends. Drew and I are the only basketball players there so it's important that we have each other's backs.

As I'm sitting on her bed, things just don't feel quite right. My mind is saying, "this is a white girl who's been drinking, and you're a black basketball player at a predominantly white institution…Get yo black self out of here!" But my manhood is saying, "relax, she's been coming on to you all night. She wants you. Plus, you've had sex with girls at parties before, this'll be no different." In that moment, my manhood was making more sense to me than my mind. Back then I believed that true manhood was found in the number of women a man lied down with, and just when I decided to take this situation a step further, Drew busted open the door. "Breeze we gotta go!" He seemed like he was in a panic, so I figured it was serious. I jumped in my Adidas, and we left, taking notice of all the dirty looks her friends gave me on the way out.

"What was going on back there?" I asked Drew as we stepped in the elevator. "All of her friends were out there saying, 'this is wrong, he shouldn't be in there with her.' Like, I know she was coming on to you all night, and they knew it to, but it just looked bad. So, I had to get you out of there." Usually, I was the one who made those type of heads-up decisions. I was the one who peeped every detail and weighed my options before making a move, but not that night. I allowed my "manhood" to put me in a situation that could have been extremely detrimental. I was starting to slip, and this was only the beginning.

Georgia Tech was our third game of the year and Coach Ingle had been telling me about this game since he started recruiting me. "I'm not worried about Georgia Tech" he would say. "We're gonna beat them! I'm more worried about the next game when we play University of Tennessee Chattanooga!" Georgia Tech played in the ACC, which was considered the toughest conference for college basketball at the time. They were known for putting together solid teams and kept a future NBA player or two. Matter of fact, the team we'd be playing had Iman Shumpert, who would be a first round draft pick for the New York Knicks the following year. I didn't see why Coach Ingle would be more focused on Tennessee Chattanooga than them. "After you guys beat Tech, y'all are gonna get the big head, and Tennessee Chattanooga is gonna sneak right up on you." I couldn't see that happening. Coach Hartry, my high school coach, had a saying, "You kill an ant with a sledgehammer!" The logic behind that was, you could probably kill an ant by flicking it, or putting a pressure on it with your thumb, right? Well, if you crushed it with a sledgehammer, you were making a statement and letting the ant know you're nothing to be played with. Translation, if you're better than a team, don't play around with them, crush them early and let it be known.

Coach Matta had talked to me about this game a couple times too, but right before I got to school, he decided that he wasn't going to coach at Kennesaw; Instead, he would coach at the local high school where his son played. I was disappointed because I was looking forward to that relationship and being able to learn from him, but that's just how the game goes.

Lo and behold, we beat Georgia Tech 80-63 at home on TV. The gym was at capacity and the atmosphere was electric. It was my first "big time" college game and I had made some solid contributions in the win. We all felt good about this one and we enjoyed it for sure. Then we played Tennessee Chattanooga a couple days later. We were surprised to come out of the locker room and barely see anyone in the stands. We just had a packed house the other night and now no one was there. It didn't make sense, but it didn't matter either. We took down perennial powerhouse Georgia Tech and we thought that we were going to absolutely smash Tennessee Chattanooga. On paper, we had them beat; and when I saw them during warmups, all I could think about was killing an ant with a sledgehammer. All my teammates felt the same way.

They shocked us that night though, beating us 79-63, in our gym just like Coach Ingle had said. We didn't look like the same team that beat Georgia Tech a couple nights earlier. We made a lot of mental mistakes and played selfishly, and with arrogance. When we got in the locker room, Coach Ingle didn't have a lot to say. I don't even remember too much of what he said, it was basically along the lines of, "I told you so." I looked at Coach Ingle like he was a prophet.

From there, we went on a ten-game losing streak, and you can probably imagine that no one was too happy about that. A team that was extremely talented from top to bottom and started the season off with so much promise, was now in a severe drought. This losing streak exposed a lot of what was wrong with our team. There were rifts between players from things that happened off the court which eventually spilled onto the court. The team basically was split into two factions. However, the three freshmen, Nick, Drew, and I, we called ourselves, "The Big 3", stuck together like glue. We'd sit around and play video games (preferably NBA 2k), and party during our free time to clear our heads. But often times, that didn't give me the relief that I was looking for; It only suppressed my issues, and I was looking for another way to deal with the everything that was going on in my mind.

Adrian and I had been dating since my sophomore year of high school. She was a year older than me, therefore she went to college before me. When my senior year of high school started, which was her freshman year of college, we decided to do the long-distance thing, and at first, we made it work, but I could see that it wasn't sustainable. I was the first person she had been with, but now that she was in college, she wanted to explore and see what else was out there. "I need to see if you and I are right." I wish she would have just been straight up with me and said, "I met this guy, and I kinda like him. Oh, and I want to have sex with him too." I would have respected her so much more if she would have done that, but that wasn't the route she chose, and I would eventually catch wind of what she was doing. To be honest, it hurt me pretty bad and made me feel as though I was less of a man. And since my manhood was threatened, the only thing I knew to do was retaliate. At the time, I believed that if someone hurts you, you hurt them worse. Years later I would hear a phrase that would send shockwaves throughout my mind, "hurt people, hurt people." I cheated on her for the rest of my senior year, with each interaction I would extract my revenge, but it felt as though I could never get enough to heal the wounds that marred my heart. That annoyed me because in retrospect I realize that all I wanted to do was heal, but I CHOSE to hurt. Even though my disdain was beginning to grow for her, when she came home for holiday breaks and things like that, we were the perfect couple. The perfect toxic couple.

Now that I was in college and surrounded by even more women, things got worse. I could tell that Adrian felt as though she was losing me. And she was. In an attempt to salvage what we had, she would schedule phone and video calls at night, but I always had an excuse as to why I couldn't talk. Even when she came back home to visit, I rarely made time to see her. She had hurt me, and I was still harboring those feelings. Along with those feelings, was a deep fear. A fear of not being accepted. I wanted everyone to like me, so at times I wouldn't say or do things that needed to be said or done in fear of hurting someone's feelings and them not liking me. I actually cared what people thought about me, even though I acted as if I didn't. My image was so important to me that at times it imprisoned me in a place of timidity. But sex, sex helped me dull my pain and my fears. It helped me find the relief that video games and partying didn't. During sex, there was nothing to be afraid of, there was only pleasure to look forward to. When I was lost in a state of bliss and passion with a woman, I felt as though I was at home; I felt complete, and I started to look at sex, not only as a pleasurable act, but as a part of me.

Even though I was struggling to fully piece together my identity off the court, basketball still felt right. The game was still that guiding light that was trying to keep me from being fully submerged into the darkness of my personal life. Basketball was still pure in my eyes, but I would soon come to the realization that basketball on that level was more than just playing a game. It was a result driven business.

Business

"Do not be misled: Bad company corrupts good character."
(1 Corinthians 15:33 NIV)

My Dad would often say, "this is a business" when he referred to basketball, and it took me a while to fully understand what he meant. I remember going out of town for AAU games; Him, Coach Rob, and Coach C would be sure to tell us before we got in the fifteen-passenger van, "this is a business trip fellas." They viewed it as an opportunity for us to showcase our talent, while we viewed it as a vacation where we got to play a few basketball games. I still saw basketball as this beautiful and fun game, but there was another side to the game that I had not yet been introduced to. A grimy side. A side so repulsive, it was enough to make you walk away from the game for good.

I first began to notice this other side of basketball during NBA Playoff games. "This ain't even real basketball anymore, this is sports entertainment", is what my dad would say as we watched those games together. I started to notice how the NBA seemed to want those playoff series to be stretched out. More games, equals more money. There was nothing wrong with that because the NBA is a business, but it seemed as though it wasn't about the Love of the game anymore. It was more so about making money.

Then around 2010, a brand emerged on the basketball scene that absolutely came and took over. Ball Is Life. It was the perfect description of how people felt about basketball. It described how I felt about basketball. Unfortunately, it reminded me of my suicide attempts from my middle school days too. Basketball was everything to me, and if I couldn't play it, I'd rather die. Judging by the way people responded to the brand, I wasn't the only one who felt that way. Ball Is Life helped spread AAU and high school basketball by putting together content in the form of highlights for some of the nation's top players. They also had merchandise like backpacks and socks. It was honestly a genius idea, and it was beautiful watching it blossom the way it did. But some players, coaches, and people who were highly involved with basketball only cared about the social media views and cashing in, and I'm not saying there's anything wrong with that. What I am saying is that I began to see a shift in basketball. Some coaches were no longer interested in the development of players, they were just looking to get paid. Now that I was in college, I was seeing basketball evolve from this beautiful game that brought me passion and excitement, into this currency driven leviathan.

Regardless of the shift, I did my best to hold on to the belief that basketball was still the same game that I fell in Love with all those years ago. But in March of 2011, just after my freshman season ended, I saw first-hand that this game was different at this level. This game was about results, and if you couldn't produce, you would be replaced.

We lost to Belmont in the first round of our conference tournament. Belmont was one of those teams that would set all the right screens, communicate perfectly on defense, and just absolutely destroy you with fundamentally sound basketball. There would be no dunking, no flashy passes, just fundamental basketball that beat you every time. I hated playing teams like that because they would make you pay for every mistake you made. Anyway, our season was over, and I was packing some things into a duffle bag to head back to Tucker for spring break when my phone rang. I don't remember who called me, but I'll never forget what they said. "Yo! Coach Ingle just got fired!"

We went 8-23 that season, and the powers that be felt as though it was time for a change. Over the past few years, there had been some complaints about the basketball players smoking weed, drinking, and not going to class, and they felt that Coach Ingle had lost control of the program. The losing season was the cherry on top and they had everything they needed to push him out. Coach Ingle was a motivator. He was one of those coaches that you would run through a wall for because you knew that he'd do anything for you. They just didn't think Coach Ingle could get it done anymore, and at this level they didn't care about how good of a guy he was, they wanted results. But Coach Ingle was resilient, and he showed them that he could still get it done. He went down the road to Dalton State University and won a national championship two seasons later. But throughout that ordeal is when I started to realize this just wasn't basketball anymore, this was a business.

I had gained twenty-five pounds my freshman year going from 220lbs to 245lbs by the end of the season. I listened to what some of my older teammates were saying about the changes that a new coach would possibly be making when he came in. "He's probably gonna cut some of us so he can bring in the players he wants…" At first, I didn't think it was likely, but after I took into consideration how they just gave Coach Ingle the boot, a guy who would have given his life for this program, I knew anything was possible. I Loved Kennesaw, it was home, and I didn't want to give the new coach any reason to cut me; So, I decided it was in my best interest to get back into shape. You're probably thinking, "how can a college athlete be out of shape when you're working out majority of the time?" I'll be the first one to tell you that being in shape has so much more to do with than just working out. We worked out every day since I stepped on campus, and I still managed to gain weight. Working out is important, but what you eat plays an even bigger role; So, my diet was the first place I decided to make changes. I cut out fried foods, red meat, sweets, and alcohol (well I didn't fully cut out alcohol). I also put in extra work on the court and in the weight room. During the few weeks this was going on, the Athletic Department had been searching for a new coach and had narrowed it down to four candidates: Mark Price, Corey Williams, Greg Matta, and Lewis Preston.

The athletic director called us down to the gym one afternoon. He told us about the candidates and informed us that he and the powers that be wanted us to be active participants in this decision-making process. We took that as we were going to have the final say in who we wanted to be our coach. It made sense to us because ultimately, we'd be spending the most time with him and it needed to be someone that we were comfortable with and wanted to play for, right? Wrong. A collegiate institution was getting ready to bring in a coach that they would pay hundreds of thousands of dollars and could possibly bring in millions for the school, and we thought they would leave a decision like that up to a group of 18-22 year old kids. How naïve. When they said active participants, this is what they meant. "We're going to allow you guys to sit down with the candidates and interview with them and ask them any questions you'd like. And when you're all done, you're going to vote on who you want to be your coach. It won't really matter though because we already know who we're going to pick, but this will be a fun exercise anyway."

The first candidate we sat down with was Mark Price. He was a Georgia Tech alumnus and played twelve years in the NBA. He was known as one of the best shooters to ever play the game. We were all excited about the possibility of him being our coach, but there were rumors going around that he was ultimately just trying to get to his alma mater, and Kennesaw was just a steppingstone. I didn't want to believe that, but his interview proved that there might be some truth behind it. I don't know if it was just his personality, but it seemed as though he didn't really want to be there. He was flat and answered our questions in a very monotone like voice. None of us were feelin' him.

Within the next couple days, we sat down with Corey Williams. He was an assistant at Florida State University and played in the NBA for the Chicago Bulls in the early nineties. Yes, that means he played with Michael Jordan. Our sit down with him went well. He was a good guy, but he wasn't the right fit for us. Some of my teammates joked that he could possibly get us hooked up with all kinds of sneakers from Michael Jordan though. That would have actually been pretty cool, but this was bigger than sneakers. Our immediate futures and our dreams were at stake; And we knew the last two candidates were the ones that the athletic director and the powers that be were considering the most. It would ultimately come down to one of these two.

The first thing I noticed about Lewis Preston was his height. He was 6'9. "If he gets the job, he'll be the tallest coach I've ever had," I said to myself as he walked into the room. He had an impressive resume to go along with his height. He played college basketball at VMI and then went on to have a successful professional career overseas. The University of Florida had won national championships back to back from 2005-2006 and 2006-2007, he coached there during the latter. He had been a part of the development of guys like Joakim Noah, Corey Brewer, and Al Horford who were in the middle of flourishing NBA careers. At the time of the interview, he was at Penn State where he was enjoying a fruitful career as well. I thought the interview went well, and honestly, I could see him being a good fit for us. He answered every question with class and eloquence, and it seemed as though he had done his homework on us calling us by our names. But even though he had the best interview so far, we still had one more candidate, Greg Matta.

Coach Matta was the coach that had initially recruited me to come to Kennesaw but left just before I got there because he wanted to coach his son at one of the local high schools. Everyone always told me that he left because he and Coach Ingle didn't agree on a few things, but I never bothered to find out exactly why. Coach Matta said he wanted to coach his son and that was good enough for me.

But now he had an opportunity to be in charge and we were all excited about it. All but one of us. My older teammates had all played for Coach Matta and had the same thing to say about him, "he's the kinda coach you'd run through a wall for." Nick wasn't sold on the idea though. He understood how everyone felt, but he wanted to make sure that our next coach would be someone who could lead this program in the right direction. He was leaning towards getting someone fresh in there, someone who would bring a new culture to the program. He and everyone else outside of our team thought it might be best to get someone in there who wouldn't carry any remnants of the previous regime. I understood that. I didn't agree with it, but I understood.

Out of all the interviews, Coach Matta's was the most genuine. That room was filled with such optimism and enthusiasm, as opposed to the previous interviews where it was filled with unease and anxiousness. We were all just as excited as kids the night before Christmas. Coach Matta was smooth, and extremely cool, and we knew that this was the right fit. After the interview, I went up to him and shook his hand just as he exited the room. He firmly grasped my hand and winked at me. I felt as though something great was on the horizon, like the part of the Rocky movies where the theme music starts playing and Sylvester Stallone goes into the training montage. We walked out of that room hopeful and expectant that they would announce Greg Matta as the next head men's basketball coach at Kennesaw State University.

The next day we sat down with the athletic director, and he asked us who we liked the best out of the four candidates. There was a moment of silence as we looked around the rectangular conference table at one another making sure that we were all on the same page. Then we said in unison, "Matta." All but one of us. Nick had class when we interviewed Coach Matta, therefore he couldn't be there. So, when the athletic director asked who we liked the best, Nick not being one to hold his tongue, let him know his concerns about bringing in someone who had already been there to be the new head coach. I'm sure if he would have met Coach Matta, he would've felt another way.

About a week later, a group of us were eating in the cafeteria, and a student comes up to us and says, "congrats on your new coach." We looked at each other confused and asked what he was talking about. He told us that he heard we had a new coach, but didn't know his name. Then he walked away. We got up and walked outside where another one of our teammates walked up and showed us a Facebook article that read, "Lewis Preston named Kennesaw State Basketball Coach."

We had been told that we were going to be "instrumental" in this decision-making process, and that they wouldn't make a decision without us. Now we were finding out through social media, and that created a rift between us and the athletic department. Yeah, we wanted Coach Matta, but it wasn't the fact that they didn't choose him, it was the way they went about it. They treated us like we were the public instead of the ones who would be most affected by this decision. We felt betrayed.

The next day we were called into one of those fancy meeting rooms in the registrar's office. We knew that they were going to introduce us to our new coach and the gloomy afternoon set the stage as we took our time getting to the building. We were all hoping that the article was a fake and that Coach Matta would be our coach, but as we turned the corner to enter the room, we saw Lewis Preston's 6'9 frame at the opposite end of the hallway. Tension, anxiety, and anger simmered in the room to create a somber mood as we waited for our new coach to enter. No one knew what his first act would be as head coach. For all we knew, he could come in there and say, "I'm bringing in my own players, all of you need to transfer."

From my experience, first impressions can make or break a relationship. Often times when you think about someone, the first time you met them comes to mind. I knew this meeting would be crucial for us and our new coach. The door handle turned and Vaughn Williams, the athletic director, walked in. He throws on a smile and says, "Good afternoon fellas" as he rubs his hands together. No one greeted him. He pauses in the awkward silence and goes on to say, "I know by now all of you have probably heard that we've named Lewis Preston as your new head coach." "Man, you lied to us!" Spencer Dixon, our fearless point guard interrupts. "You said that we would be instrumental in the decision-making process, and you didn't even take into consideration what we said!" Spencer was right, they did lie to us. "Listen, we took your thoughts into consideration, but we thought this was the best move for the program." It was tough to hear, but we had to realize our complaints wouldn't bring about any change. The decision was final.

After a few more minutes of answering questions, Vaughn Williams walked out, and Coach Preston walked in. He took off his suit jacket, layed it across the back of his chair, sat down and said, "As I look around the room, I see a lot of long faces. I know you guys were pulling for someone else, but all I ask is that you give me a chance." At this point it's not like we could change anything, we were either going to play for him or have to find somewhere else to play. Then he went around the room, "Markeith? Aaron? Drew? Breeze?..." We all nodded our heads as to say, "Yes, we'll give you a fair shot." He didn't do anything to us, he was just a man going after his dream of being a collegiate head coach. He deserved a fair chance.

Everyone wasn't joining in on this kumbaya moment though. There were still a few that were pretty upset about the decision. And as Coach Preston talked to us, tempers flared. "That's why I heard you got kicked out of Florida for messing with some girls!" one teammate yelled. I was just as disappointed as some of my other teammates that Coach Matta didn't get the job, but I couldn't believe a moment that had the potential for such a beautiful outcome had turned into an attempt to chop this man down. Coach Preston smirked and sat on the edge of his seat and said in one of the coolest and calmest tones you can imagine, "We'll just see what Al Horford has to say about me in my press release."

A Dirty Game

"First clean the inside of the cup and the plate, that the outside also may be clean."
(Matthew 23:26 ESV)

By the time summer workouts began I was down to 233lbs. Things were moving in the right direction, but I still wasn't where I wanted to be. I was someone who had always been image conscious, how I looked was important to me. So much so that during this time if I ate something that I shouldn't have eaten, I would almost immediately slip away to stick my fingers down my throat. See, my image and my identity were intertwined. If I didn't look the way I wanted to look, I had a negative view of myself. I think many people feel the same way, which isn't true at all. It's just a tactic satan uses to make us feel as though we aren't good enough. When in reality, what Jesus did for us made us more than good enough; but I didn't know that at the time and throwing up food that wasn't good for me was my way of managing my image, identity, and my weight. I thought it was harmless at first, but it ended up being something that I would struggle with for the next six years of my life.

That summer, I made a promise to myself that I would do every rep in every workout. I promised myself that I would touch every line on every sprint. I promised myself that I wouldn't cut any corners, and that I would push myself to the limit. I didn't care what I had to do, I just wanted to get better. When summer workouts and summer school ended, I decided to go to Indiana with Nick. Nick was a basketball savant. There wasn't a player he didn't know about, and there wasn't a move he couldn't do on the court. When he invited me to come up to Indianapolis and train with him and spend some time with his family, I jumped at the opportunity. His dad, Greg Turner, played collegiately at Auburn with Charles Barkley, and was drafted into the NBA. He would always give me tips when he came to see us play our freshman year, and I was looking forward to any knowledge he would share during my time there.

We spent a week in Indiana. Nick showed me around his hometown, and we trained 2-3 times a day. A session in the morning, a session in the afternoon, and sometimes a light session in the evening. To me there was nothing more enjoyable than working on your game in a hot gym on a summer day. It was almost as if you could feel yourself getting better, and sometimes I enjoyed that more than playing in the actual game. Nick's family showed me so much Love while I was there, which made the trip even better. I'm a firm believer that being around good people is good for your health.

I had high hopes going into my sophomore season. I was down to 205lbs, meaning I had shed 40lbs in seven months. I looked and felt like a different person and player. This was a new season, with a new coaching staff with new goals, but I still had the same struggles on and off the court.

On the court, I struggled with consistency. Growing up, I would have games where it looked like I was the best player in the country, and then turn around a have a game where it didn't look like I belonged on a basketball court. My dad would always say, "You gotta be able to put a string of games together man." But consistency is tough. It takes a tough person to show up every day and perform, whether it be basketball, school, business or relationships. Consistent people are the ones who can block out all the outside noise and focus to get the job done. That was a skill that I hadn't yet mastered.

I started the season well, but I hit a rough patch, and about midway through, I was beginning to lose my confidence; and you never want to do that, as a person or as a basketball player. I had been through rough patches with the game before, all players have; the only way to get through it, is to go through it. You've just got to keep playing and keep believing that it's going to turn around. All it takes is one play to give you the boost you're looking for, but it was so much easier said than done. During those times, every mistake you make is amplified, and holds more weight than the last. You start to doubt yourself, and the game begins to feel like a chore. I found comfort in the game, I also tried to find my identity in the game, so, when I wasn't playing well, it not only affected me on the court, but in my personal life also.

With my confidence dwindling, I began to desperately search for ways to boost it. I turned to the thing that always seemed to lift my spirit, sex. Sex represented enjoyment and adventure, yet now I was using it to find myself and my confidence. But in this attempt to find those things, I was actually giving pieces of me away to every woman that I slept with. Before long, I started to notice a change within myself; I felt empty. I had an even-tempered nature, but now I was easily frustrated by things that I would have once brushed off. Nothing that I was doing was working and, in my desperation, I decided to get back to the basics during the last stretch of the season. I started reading the Bible verses my mom had given me again, along with listening to Pastor Dollar in the morning before class and on gamedays. In the evenings, I would go to the gym to get shots up alone. I Loved being in the gym late at night by myself. When it was full, it was my stage, but when it was empty, it was my sanctuary.

During that last stretch of the season, I played the best I had played all year. It was like I hit the reset button; Not only did I feel like myself again, but I was playing like myself again. I had gotten through the rough patch, but it wasn't because I went about doing things my way; My way only brought me confusion. It was because I surrendered to the only one who could get me through, God. I could feel God calling me to walk away from the lifestyle that was slowing me down, but I just wasn't ready. I still wanted to party. I still wanted to find myself before I came to Him. But little did I know that the only place where I could find myself, was in Him.

We finished the season with a 3-27 record. They gave Coach Preston the benefit of the doubt because he was still working with the players from the Ingle Regime. He was only able to bring in one player his first year. I took that personally because they made it seem like Coach Ingle's guys couldn't cut it, and that just wasn't true.

Everyone is always going to have an opinion, especially about a team that just went 3-27. Personally, I believe there was a disconnect between the coaches and the players. They didn't like our style of play, and we didn't like the way they coached. I've played basketball all around the country, and it's played differently everywhere you go. In the south, the game was based on athleticism and strength, in the north ball handling was emphasized, and on the west coast it was all run and gun. Our coaches were from the Midwest where they liked to slow things down, set a bunch of screens, and run your offense. Most of us were from the south and that wasn't the type of game that complimented our skillset. Also, Coach Preston would pull us out whenever we made a mistake. It made us feel like we were walking or playing on eggshells. Every time one of us made a mistake, we immediately looked to the scorer's table because we knew someone was coming in for us. As players, we didn't have the chance to grow if we weren't able to play through our mistakes. Not only were mistakes apart of the game, but they were apart of life. That was the most frustrating part about playing for Coach Preston that season. But during that last stretch, I became accustomed to his coaching style and was able to find places where I could be successful in his system. I ended the season on a high note and made a promise to myself that next season I wouldn't need time to get adjusted; I planned to hit the ground running.

It was April 2012, and we were in the apartment playing NBA 2K, enjoying ourselves as usual when Nick gets a call from one of our coaches. They needed him to come down to the basketball office. He grabbed his backpack and walked out. He had been acting a bit different for about a week or so, but I couldn't quite figure out what was going on with him. He didn't want to come to the cafeteria and eat with us or go hang out on campus. I figured he just needed some time to himself, and he would open up to us when he was ready. He returned a couple hours later and said, "they let me go." "What you mean they let you go!?" I asked in confusion. "They don't want me to come back next year. I suspected they might do something like this." Then it all made sense and I understood why he had been acting different. He knew this was coming.

Back in January, I had tickets to an Atlanta Hawks game one night, and Nick was going with me. The game was at 7pm and the plan was for him to go and kick it at his girlfriend's house and be back around 6pm so we could leave on time. He calls me around 5:50pm and says, "I'm not feeling too well man, I'm gonna sit this one out." I'm thinking ok, his girl has persuaded him to stay with her. No problem, I know how it goes. But I was also thinking, "You do know we're broke college students, and we have great seats, it might be a minute before I get these tickets again. Don't be dumb, she's gonna be there after the game!" But I didn't say that to him. I just said, "that's cool" and invited Drew. He gets dressed in a flash and we head downtown. I was excited because my favorite player, Tracy McGrady, had signed with the Hawks that summer and this would be my first time seeing him play in person since my freshman year of high school.

We have a great time at the game, Tracy McGrady plays great, and the Hawks win; I couldn't ask for a better night. On the way back, I get a call from Nick's girlfriend who sounds a bit concerned. "Hey, Nick isn't feeling well and says he wants to go to the hospital." "What's wrong?" I asked. "We got some food and he started saying that his stomach was hurting." "Ok, give me a sec, I'll call you back."

At this point, I feel like I have to make a decision. When someone is asking to go to the hospital, that means it's usually pretty serious. I'm also thinking it might be food poisoning. I decide call our team trainer. "Hey what's up, Nick isn't feeling good and wants to go to the hospital." "What did he eat?" She asked. "A burger and fries this one place" (Can't name the restaurant, don't want to risk getting sued). "Well, it sounds like food poisoning. I don't think he needs to go to the hospital; he probably just needs to lie down. Plus, we leave pretty early tomorrow," she said. We had a game at USC Upstate in two days and would be leaving tomorrow morning. "Ok, we'll keep an eye on him."

When we got back to the apartment, nick and his girlfriend are there. He's lying down and she steps out of his room to tell us what happened. "He ate a burger, and then not long after said that his stomach was hurting." I peered back in the room at Nick. He was knocked out and seemed to be alright. "He seems to be ok right now and I don't want to wake him" I said. "Let's just keep an eye on him through the night."

The next day came and Nick was still in pain. We all pack up and leave to go to the team bus. Our trainer examines him before we get on and gives him something to help his stomach. Then we leave for South Carolina.

The following day was game day, and I remember everyone out on the court warming up, except Nick. I knew something was wrong because he hadn't said much the past few days which was extremely out of the ordinary for him. As we're in the layup line, Nick comes out of the locker room, in his uniform, hunched over, holding his stomach, and barely moving. All of us, including the coaches, knew there was no way he could play this game.

After we lost, we boarded the bus and went to our next destination, Johnson City, Tennessee, to play East Tennessee State University. It was about a three-hour ride. When we arrived, it was around 8pm and we were all hungry. We walked to a restaurant that was just down the street from our hotel. Nick was with us, and he couldn't eat, he just put his head down on the table while the rest of us stuffed our faces; matter of fact, we had to help him walk to and from the restaurant.

When we came down for breakfast the next morning, Coach Preston and Coach Lallathin pulled Drew and I aside. "Nick is in the hospital. We decided to take him last night. There was something going on with his appendix." I didn't know much about the appendix, but it sounded serious. "He's having emergency surgery, but he'll be fine. We're going to bring you guys by the hospital to see him after the game."

After the game that night (we lost by the way) we made our way to the hospital. We walk in to see Nick awake, lying in bed and watching tv. Seeing everyone lifted his spirits, but I could also tell that he didn't like being seen lying in a hospital bed either. He told us that he had watched the game on his laptop, and it was a game that he should have won. We had chances to win lots of the games that we lost that season; it was always the small things that made the difference. Missed rebound, missed free throw, missed layup.

When it was time to leave and get back on the road to Georgia, everyone left, but Drew and I hung back for a sec because Nick had something to tell us. "The doctors said if I had waited any longer to come in, my appendix was going to burst, and I would have died."

Nick had grown to become my best friend and the thought of losing him was something that I didn't want to face. I partially blamed myself for him being in that hospital bed. I should have disregarded what our trainer said and taken him to the hospital when I came back from the Hawks game. I learned a valuable lesson that night, if someone asks to go to the hospital, TAKE THEM.

Nick wouldn't play another game that season, and now the coaching staff was releasing him after he almost lost his life on their watch. Not to mention Nick's grandfather passed at the beginning of the season and he still came out and practiced every day, including the day that he found out. To release him was heartless in my opinion. Because of this, I began to build up a distaste for Coach Preston and his staff. I saw that this wasn't a family, like many of the other teams I had played on in the past. This was a business, and I was just another employee; and If I didn't consistently perform, I would be replaced too.

The situation with Nick not only changed the way I viewed our coaching staff, but basketball as well. The game was once so pure and beautiful to me, and all I wanted to do was protect it. But now I was seeing how this part of the game lacked compassion and humanity. I thought about Sharisse and how I would see her dribble the ball up the hill to go play at the park, and I thought about the first time I saw my dad play. Back then, basketball was so virtuous and life giving. My hope was that it would stay that way for as long as I was a part of it; but I was naïve to think something so beautiful could withstand the test of time. I was foolish for thinking that something could remain pure in this corrupt world. Yet I often wondered, was basketball a dirty game, or was it the people in it who were dirty?

The Drift

"So we must listen very carefully to the truth we've heard, or we may drift away from it."

(Hebrews 2:1 NLT)

We're all shaped by the things we go through, good or bad; and sometimes no matter how much we resist the change, it's inevitable. Going into my junior year, I could feel myself go through a shift. Up to that point, my first two years of college had been amazing. Even when times got rough with basketball, I still looked forward to my time off the court. But now anger and contempt began infiltrate my once joyful soul. Adrian and I had officially called it quits. Our relationship was a sham, and it was time to let it go. I felt like I couldn't trust my coaches, and I had seen my best friend forced out of our school, which marked the beginning of the end for "The Big 3." I think what hurt the most was finally finding a group of people where I felt like I belonged, and to see it broken up so unfairly just wasn't right. But I was a master at concealing my emotions. It was easy to hide behind a mask, I had done it my whole life. And that summer, I hid behind the same four masks that I had grown accustomed to: sex, weed, alcohol, and basketball.

I accepted a weird friend request on Facebook one day from a guy that I didn't know. His profile picture showed a woman kissing his head, and as I went through his pictures, I noticed that he seemed to be with different women quite often. I'm not sure why I accepted the friend request, but I felt like I didn't have a reason not to accept it either. A couple days later he sends me a message. "What's up?". I chose not to respond. The next day he sends the same message, "What's up?". Again, I chose not to respond. He sends the same message a couple days later, "What's up?". This time I replied, "Yo, what's going on man?" "Nothing much, just chillin outside of this private party in Buckhead. What's good on your end?" He quickly answered back. "Nothing much man, probably about to call it a night," I replied. At this point I'm thinking this dude is weird and was contemplating blocking him.

Then he sends another message, "You're about to call it a night this early? The sun ain't even up lol. Half the people at this orgy haven't even shown up yet…"

Orgy? He had my attention.

The story of Samson was one of the first stories I remember my mom reading to us when we were kids, and quickly became one of my favorites. For those who aren't familiar with the story, Samson was one of the judges of Israel and a legendary warrior. He was like Superman, or Superman was like him, but he couldn't fly or shoot lasers from his eyes; well, The Bible doesn't say he could, but you never know.

His purpose was to use his strength and fighting prowess to set the Israelites free from the oppression of the Philistines. Samson was strong and killed a lion with his bare hands and once killed 1,000 men with the jawbone of a dead donkey. But even though Samson had all this strength and fighting skill, he had a weakness…kryptonite, I mean...women.

Samson's people, the Israelites, were at odds with the Philistines, but he was attracted their women. He fell in Love with a Philistine woman named Deliah. The leaders of the Philistines told Deliah to entice Samson and find out the secret to his strength so they could kill him. Her reward for this betrayal would be 1,000 pieces of silver which would be between $250,000 - $300,000 today.

Deliah goes to Samson and says, "please tell me what makes you so strong and what it would take to tie you up securely." I don't know about Samson, but if a woman asked me how I can be tied up securely, I'd be extremely cautious of her; but he replies, "If I were tied up with seven new bowstrings that have not been dried yet I would become as weak as anyone else." She had hidden some of the Philistine men in her house and after tying him up with seven new bowstrings, she then yells, "Samson! The Philistines have come to capture you!" But he breaks the strings easily.

She comes back again and says, "You've been making fun of me and telling me lies! Now please tell me how you can be tied up securely." He replies, "If I were tied up with brand new ropes that had never been used, I would become as weak as anyone else." Again, Delilah had hidden some of the Philistine men in her home as she begins to tie him up. She then cried out, "Samson! The Philistines have come to capture you!" But again, Samson snaps the ropes as if they were thread.

Still motivated by the money, Delilah asks Samson again about the secret to his strength. "If you were to weave the seven braids in my hair into the fabric on your loom and tighten it, I would become as weak as anyone else." Then she waited until he fell asleep and weaved his hair into the fabric on her loom. With the Philistine men hiding out in her house, she yelled out the phrase that pays, "Samson! The Philistines have come to capture you!" Samson wakes up and yanks his hair from the loom.

Frustrated and desperate, she pulls out the big guns. She hits Samson with the "L" word. "How can you tell me you Love me if you don't share your secrets with me!?" Samson should have known something was up because this lady was so pressed to find out his weakness. Finally, Samson tells her his secret, "my hair has never been cut." See, God had shown himself to Samson's parents before he was born and He told them that you will have a son and gave them some instructions for him, one of which was to never cut his hair.

When Samson told Delilah that, she knew that he had finally been honest with her. She lulled him to sleep and had someone come in to shave his head; and his hair fell to the ground, so did his strength. Then she tied him up and yelled out the magical words. He woke up but wasn't able to break out of the restraints. Then the Philistines rushed in, gouged out his eyes and hauled him off to their hideout where they imprisoned Samson for some time.

Now the Philistines were having a party and celebrating the fact that they've finally defeated their greatest foe. Blinded and in chains, they brought Samson out to amuse them and had him stand between the pillars that supported the roof. The party was packed with about 3,000 people, but Samson's hair had started to grow back. As he stood against the supporting pillars he prayed, "Lord, remember me. Give me strength just one more time so I can pay back the Philistines for the loss of my eyes." He pushed over the supporting pillars and the building collapsed, killing himself and all the Philistines in the temple that day.

I related to Samson in a lot of ways, not the killing a lion with my bare hand's kind of ways; but the women were my weakness kind of ways. If you ask me, Samson was blind before the Philistines gouged out his eyes. He couldn't see through Delilah's tricks (I'm going to ask him about that when I get to Heaven). I was no different. At times I would be so caught up with women and sex that I would disregard my responsibilities. Some nights, I would stay up late kickin' it with different women, when I should have been in bed getting some rest for the game the next day. My priorities were off, and I knew it, but I CHOSE to ignore the warning signs, much like Samson.

Now, this guy on Facebook was telling me about these orgy parties that he threw, and I'm not going to lie, I was interested. I still held on to the belief that true manhood was found in the number of women you lied down with, and I was still looking for the real Brandon Dawson. As we continued to message, he informed me that he was a pornographic filmmaker and that he thought I had a look that could make me some money in his line of work. But I would need to come out to the parties before we got to that step.

He told me about the process, and I was all in. The only thing I had to do was build my profile on his site, go get tested, and start "partying", but something was off. I felt something deep within me telling me not to go through with this. It was much like that day outside my house with the antifreeze bottle. I didn't hear an audible voice, but somehow, I knew that if I were to do this, there might not be any coming back from it.

I turned down his offer.

The fact that I had even considered that lifestyle let me know that I was drifting. I was drifting from God and my upbring, and honestly it scared me. How far was I willing to go to find out who the real Brandon Dawson was? What was I willing to do? Was this even about finding myself anymore, or had I become addicted to sex? Drifting isn't something that happens overnight, it's a gradual process. It starts by doing "little" things like watching porn and skipping school to have sex. Before you know it, you're so far out that you can't see the coastline anymore. I felt like I was in the ocean at night and the current was pulling me further and further from the coast. This wasn't the first time I felt like that, nor would it be the last, but basketball was my lighthouse. Whenever I felt the current of life pulling me out to sea, basketball was always able to guide me back to what was real. But now that light was going dim, and every time I found myself drifting, it became a bit more difficult to make it back to shore.

A Bad Mix

"For am I now seeking the approval of man, or of God? Or am I trying to please man?"

(Galatians 1:10 ESV)

I tore my meniscus playing in the Wallace Prather Pro-Am the summer going into my junior year. Meniscus tears sound serious but are common and can be repaired surgically or heal on their own in some cases. In my case, the doctors thought it was best to go the surgery route since it was the summer, and we had a few months before the season began. The surgery was scheduled towards the end of July which was about a month out.

I had never been under the knife. I had always heard that players weren't the same after surgery, and Mike, our trainer could see the concerned plastered all over my face as we left the doctor's office. "Ya know, at my old school, we had a guy come back from a meniscus injury in about ten days." He went on to say, "the plan is to get your knee and the surrounding muscles as strong as it can get within a month's time frame, that way recovery won't be so tough." So, he put me through exercises and stretches six days a week right up until the time of surgery.

A year earlier Markeith busted into our apartment. He had a knack for just showing up unannounced. He and I had a running prank where we would just show up, trash each other's rooms and run out. Sometimes, he would just show up and say, "get your gear, it's time to go work out", this was one of those times. He and I went running around campus. The campus was 602 acres, which is close to a mile; so it wasn't a lot of running, but it was blazing hot, and there were all sorts of hills. We sat down at one of the fountains when we finished. As we sat there, he told me something that I would never forget, "play your game, play to your strengths."

During that time, it wasn't just a struggle to find my identity off the court, but on it as well. Yet throughout that season I learned where I was most effective as a player and what my strengths were. Now that I had a full grasp of that and was ready to hit the ground running going into pre-season, I felt like an opportunity was being snatched away from me as I sat in the hospital room awaiting the nurse to come wheel me down to surgery. I was coming into my own and it didn't feel fair that I was now being hindered by a small piece of cartilage in the lateral side of my left knee.

I'll never forget how I felt as they brought me to the operating room. All eyes were on me as they wheeled me down and doctors and nurses lined up on both sides of the hall. I had a very uneasy feeling. As I lied on the operating table, a part of me thought that I might not wake up. I don't even remember them giving me anesthesia. I just remember seeing the bright lights of the operating room.

Physical therapy would start within the next few days, and physically speaking, it was one of the toughest things I've ever had to endure. It was like learning to use my knee all over again. For so long I felt like I was treading on thin ice. Handling the pressure of wanting to perform well in school, basketball, and doing everything in my power to find out exactly who I was. Little did I know that this surgery would be the thing that would push me through that thin layer of ice and into the hypothermic waters beneath me.

Up to this point, I had been able to manage my life. I had a 3.0 GPA, basketball was going well and my social life was flourishing. I thought I had the balance I needed, but truthfully speaking, I was barely holding on and the surgery exposed that. The rehab wasn't just tough on me physically, but mentally as well. I thought I was invincible, and for the first time in my life I realized that I wasn't. Every workout made me feel as though I might not ever be the same player again. And that was a tough pill to swallow.

During my rehab, I was prescribed oxycodone, which is a medication used to treat pain, but I used it to escape. When I was on those pills, I didn't have to think about what I was going to do if I wasn't the same player I was before. Nor did I have to think about my image or who the real Brandon Dawson was. I could just float through life. It was like the never-ending roar of the crowd after a huge dunk in a game. It was intoxicating, and I found myself getting lost in it; but intoxication isn't the place to lose yourself in and I would soon find out how dangerous this game really was.

A few weeks later school had begun, and we were back on campus. It was a Saturday and I had been running around all day. I think the only thing I had eaten was a sandwich around noon along with my medication. There were a few social gatherings happening that night and I planned on being at all of them. My rehab had been going somewhat well, I still wasn't 100%, but I was making progress.

I went to smoke a blunt with one of my homegirls, Selena. After we finished smoking, I went by the apartment of one the girls who I was talking to at that time, where I continued to smoke. Good and high, I drove back to my place, showered up, and got ready to go out with some friends. We decided to go back to Selena's house because she was having people over. When we arrived, Selena was still smoking, but now a few other people were there. I joined them in the kitchen.

They pour me a shot of rum; I drink it, then take another pull from the blunt. After a few more pulls, I start to feel a bit lightheaded, so I take a seat at the table with some of the other people in the apartment. The blunt comes back around, "Breeze, it's on you..." they called out. "I'm good man" I replied. Then Selena yells, "Ahhh there he goes being a punk again!" A couple people glance my way, waiting to see how I was going to respond. Peer pressure sets in. I smirk to keep my cool; then I get up from the table with my new Levi jeans slightly hanging off my waist and make my way to the kitchen. Throughout my life, I found myself in these moments where I felt I had to prove myself, whether it be to my parents, coaches, teammates, or friends. In these moments I had to prove that I was who I said I was, or at least who my mask portrayed me to be.

They pass me the blunt. I ash it by tapping it twice with my right index finger into a nearby red solo cup. I put it to my lips, take a deep breath, and let the smoke marinate before I crack my lips and French inhaled it through my nose (I was known for the French inhale). As I release the smoke and pass the blunt, the lightheaded feeling returns, and all strength leaves me. I black out in the middle of the kitchen. I hear people yelling, "Get his legs! Get his legs!" I open my eyes as I'm being dragged out of the kitchen. All I can see are my Levi's and my red Adidas, as the floor behind me transitions from the tile of the kitchen to the carpet of the living room. They get me to a wall, sit me up, and bombard me with questions. "Breeze, are you good?" "What's going on?"

All eyes were on me as I fought to gather my thoughts. "Was the weed to strong?" Selena asked. I looked at her like she was absolutely crazy. I didn't know exactly what caused me to black out, but I knew if I was to say the weed was too strong, it would make me look weak. Plus the weed wasn't that strong. Then one of the girls asked something that actually made sense, "When was the last time you've eaten?" Barely being able to open my mouth and speak, I say in a weak and trembling voice, "I haven't eaten since noon." It was now about 11pm. Then everyone in the room says in unison "Oh sh**." I knew what they were thinking, "you can't smoke and drink on an empty stomach." Rookie mistake, I know.

She then handed me a bottle of water and some crackers. I reach out for them with my hands shaking tremendously. The same girl then asked, "Are you taking any medications?" "Yeah, for my knee," I say in that same trembling voice. Everyone in the room is scared and thinking I was about to die. "What kind of medication?" the girl asks with deep concern. At this point, the music has stopped, and everyone is within about ten feet of me, waiting on my reply. "Oxycodone." Then everyone says in unison again, "Oh sh**!" The girl asking me questions looks in my eyes, jumps up and runs out of the room. She comes back in about twenty seconds with a plastic grocery bag and opens it right in front of me. I immediately vomit into the bag. Relief hits me instantly. That night I learned prescription medication, lack of food, weed, and alcohol don't mix. I also realized that I was willing to go beyond my limits just to prove myself to other people; a trait that could've been fatal that night, and I'm sure has been fatal to many others in the past.

The cool thing about that night was the girl who gave me the water and crackers and asked me the sensible questions went on to become a nurse. Unfortunately, the bag she placed in front of me to vomit in had a hole in it (those plastic grocery bags always have holes in them for some reason) and it got all over those new Levi's. But Levi's could be washed with water, and that would be the least of my worries. There were some fiery trials ahead that would eventually show me how much of a man I wasn't.

Black and White

"There is no longer Jew or Gentile, slave or free, male and female. For you are all one in Christ Jesus."

(Galatians 2:28 NLT)

My little brother, Josh, played football for the University of Georgia and was in his freshman year. His first game was on September 1, 2012, which was also my parents 22nd wedding anniversary; and they thought going to watch Josh play would be the perfect way to celebrate. The game was scheduled for 12pm, and it was BLAZING HOT. My dad always likes to get to football games early so he can get situated, find food, and explore before going in, so we were there around 9am.

I'd been to Atlanta Falcons games growing up, but that atmosphere was completely different than that of a Georgia Bulldogs game. You couldn't walk ten feet without hearing "GO DAWGS!" I wasn't much of a college football fan, but I could tell just from being there for an hour that people seemed to care more about college football than they did the pros. Maybe the game wasn't completely tainted, and people could still see some of the purity of the game in collegiate sports that they couldn't see on the professional level.

As we waited to hop on one of the campus buses to take us from the parking lot to the stadium, I see a girl through the sea of red Georgia Bulldog madness. She was about 5'2, light brown, with a bob cut. As she flipped her hair removing it from the view of her brown eyes,

I could see this girl's aura. She looked good and she knew it. She stood on the curb awaiting one of the buses as if she was royalty and it should have already been there waiting for her. I wanted to make my way over and talk to her, but I analyzed the situation as I often did. I figured she was probably one of the players girlfriends or something, and if she wasn't, she probably went to UGA; and Athens was just a bit too far from Kennesaw. When we got to the stadium, I noticed that she was sitting in the friends and family section with us, on the same row; but by this time, I was so bothered by the 100-degree weather that I didn't even think about approaching her.

When the game was over, the campus bus dropped us back off in the parking lot. As we made our way to the car, I heard a soft voice yell "HEY!" from a distance. I looked around and saw the girl standing on a nearby hill. She signaled for me to come over. I told my parents, "I'll catch up", and I made my way to her.

"Hey what's good?" I said in the smoothest tone that I could muster up. "What's your name?" "Olivia" she charmingly replied. "You go to school out here?" I asked. "Nah, I go to Kennesaw State. You?" I couldn't believe that this girl who I've been noticing all day just told me that she went to the same school as me. "That's crazy, I go to Kennesaw. I play ball there." I quickly whip out my phone and get her number. She goes on to tell me that she has a brother that plays football for Georgia and that her family lived in Marietta, about fifteen minutes from Kennesaw. Now it made sense that she was sitting in the friends and family section. We hug, say our goodbyes, and head our separate ways.

One of my teammates was having a get together the next day and I invited Olivia. We hadn't had much time to talk the day before and I thought this would be a good opportunity to get to know her a little better. I suspected she might be the kind of girl who was accustomed to getting her way. Like, the kind of girl who didn't like being told no, but she surprised me. Out of all the girls I'd met up to that point, she was probably the most down to Earth, and was with me just about every day after that. I wasn't looking for a girlfriend at the time, but sometimes when you're not looking for something, that's when you find it.

A few weeks later, it was a Monday and we had just finished morning workouts when Coach Preston pulled me aside. "Breeze, you have a drug test tomorrow morning at 8am." Externally, I was stoic, "thanks Coach, I'll be there," I replied. But internally I was alarmed. I would always get chosen for drug test. I think they picked me so often because they thought that I would pass, and the more drug test the basketball team passed, the better the coaching staff would look. But I was one of the players who smoked the most. Normally I wouldn't have been alarmed, because they would usually give you at least 48 hours notice; but this time I only had 24. Another reason I was alarmed was because the previous weekend was homecoming and we had just smoked six blunts on Saturday.

Passing drug test wasn't hard, but it took discipline. I had a routine, drink a lot of water and workout. I had done my research and I knew that THC, the main psychoactive compound in cannabis, stuck to fat cells. So that meant I had to burn fat and flush my system if I wanted to pass this test. I had never failed a test and I was determined to keep it that way, this one would just be a little harder because I didn't have as much time. The consequences varied for failing a drug test. If it was a school administered test, I could be suspended for a few games or face some other team regulated consequences; but if it was NCAA administered, I could lose a year of eligibility. To be honest I wasn't afraid of the coaches or the NCAA, I wanted to pass because I didn't want to disappoint my parents.

After running about five miles and drinking a couple gallons of water, I found myself sitting in a sauna wearing a full sweatsuit and sneakers trying to burn all the fat that I possibly could. The next morning, I went into the training room, took my drug test, and walked out. When the news came down that I had passed, some teammates and I decided to celebrate. Celebrate how you might ask? By smoking, of course. Normally, we would smoke on the balcony of our apartment, but this time we decided to smoke in the car, in the parking lot of some nearby apartments.

Del was a year younger than me and was from Cleveland, OH. He came in my sophomore year and had an immediate impact on the floor. He and I jumped in my car, which I had now upgraded from the sky-blue Mercury Mystique to a white Pontiac Grand Am, and went to pick another one of my teammates, Spence. Spence had finished playing the year before and was now preparing to go play overseas.

Del and I waited in front of the apartments for Spence to come out. I thought he'd be down pretty quick, so I didn't bother to park, I just pulled up to the curb on the main road. As we waited, Del starts to roll the blunt. Then we heard in a loud and thunderous voice, "MOVE YOUR CAR!" I thought it was God, or Dominic Toretto, but as I looked in my rearview, I saw that a police officer had rolled up behind us and was talking to us through the loudspeaker. I nervously put the car in gear and pull off, causing Del to waste some of the weed on the floor. We pull into a parking spot, he finishes rolling up, and we go back to pick up Spence.

The apartments we went to were less than a mile from campus. Another one of our teammates lived there and we had smoked there plenty of times. That night we listened to Curren$y and Wiz Khalifa's classic mixtape "How High" as we passed the blunt and talked about life, basketball, and everything in between. After about an hour had passed, we got hungry and decided it was time to get something to eat. As I pulled out of the parking spot and drove towards the gate of the complex, I heard a voice. It was soft, yet authoritative. "You shouldn't be driving", the voice said. I recognized this voice; I knew who it was. This was the same voice that had spoken to me years ago in the driveway. This was Jesus. When He speaks to you, He doesn't speak to your ears, He speaks to your heart; and His words seem to grab hold of it and won't let go.

I stopped just before we got to the gate of the apartment complex. "You good Breeze?" Spence asked from the backseat. My pride sets in, and I started to think about all the times I've driven drunk and high from Kennesaw, to Atlanta, to the Eastside, and back again. Now I was just a mile up the road. "Ya, I'm good man", I replied.

I pulled out onto the main road. Checkpoint by Curren$y and Wiz is playing, and my seat is leaned as far back as I can lean it and still operate the vehicle. My left wrist is draped over the steering wheel and the window is slightly cracked. It's October, so there's a chill in the air, but it's bearable. I'm in the right lane, planning to turn just after I pass through the light up ahead. I see the light. It's Green Lantern green, letting me know it's all good to keep moving forward; colors are a lot more vibrant when you're high. As we approach the intersection, I hear Wiz Khalifa,

> "No matter which way I go,
> They tell me don't take that road
> But I never put my foot on the brake oh no
> I never put my foot on the break oh no, ah no oh"

All of a sudden, it felt as though time slowed down. I glance to my right and see Del looking passed me through the driver's side window. I see panic in his eyes. Then I hear Spence yell "Woah Woah!" As I turn my head, I see lights in my peripheral, and before I even have time to react....BOOM!

A car slams into my side of my vehicle; and it feels as though I had been violently awoken from a dream. The windshield cracks, the airbags deploy, and the left wrist that was draped over the steering wheel is thrusted back into my collar bone. Smoke from the airbags fill the cabin of the car. We were hit so hard that the gear shifter was protruding from the transmission tunnel. Immediately I went into this mode that I had never been in before. It was like some sort of survival mode, and the only thing on my mind was making sure everyone was safe. I put the car in park, yank out the keys, and yell, "Are ya'll alright!?" Spence and Del are a little shaken up, but besides that they were fine. I had a burn on my left forearm from the airbag, and my collar bone was a bit sore, but I wouldn't classify those as injuries. I go to open my door to check on the other driver, but it's stuck. I'd heard about car doors being stuck after accidents and drivers being trapped. All I was thinking is that the person who hit us could be dying and in need of help, I couldn't afford to be stuck. With my adrenaline pumping, I bust the door open with my shoulder. Then I run to the other driver's car. I notice that a girl is behind the wheel. She's signaling to me that her door is stuck, but she's ok. I rip the door open like Superman to help her out of the car.

"You ok?" I ask the girl as she steps out of the crumpled Chevy Malibu. She nods her head as she breathes in deeply trying to gain her composure. "Why the f*** did you hit us!?" Del yells to the girl. She's in shock and doesn't have a response. By this time, some other drivers have called 911 and have come to check on us. Since we're all good, and this was clearly her fault, my only concern is getting the weed smell out of the car. I pull Spence to the side, "Yo, what should I do about the smell?" I asked. "What kinda spray you got in the car?" He replied. I go to the glove box and pull out a half empty can of Axe body spray. "I would spray all of that in there." Spence says. So, I did, in hopes that it would masks the smell before the cops arrived, but it only made things worse.

For most of my life I've been surrounded by black people. Decatur was predominantly black, and even though Tucker historically had more white people, there were a lot of black people there. Kennesaw was predominantly white, but it didn't matter to me. I was always going to be who I was no matter what color of people I was around, that meant I was always going to treat you with respect. But I was about to learn that not everyone felt that way. I had never been in a situation where I felt I was in danger because of my skin color. I had never been in a situation where I felt I was being racially profiled; but tonight, all that was about to change.

Two officers pull up and get out to assess the situation; both are white. One of the officers comes over and makes sure that no one is injured or needs medical attention. The girl who hit us is standing by her car while Del, Spence, and I are standing on the curb of the intersection. Del is a bit unsettled by the situation and takes a walk down the block to cool off. The officers realize that the accident was the girl's fault and give her the ticket. About five minutes later her ride comes, picks her up, and she leaves. From the time the cops arrived on the scene to the girl leaving was about fifteen minutes.

My phone is on 5%. I call my parents to let them know that we had gotten into an accident, but everyone was fine, and I would call them back. The lead officer then approaches us. "Whos' the owner of that car?" he asks. "I am", I reply. He then pulls me aside and asks ,"where's the dope?" "Dope? Officer, there's no dope in that car." Irritated by my reply, he looks at me and says, "Don't play with me, where's the dope?" "There is no dope in that car officer." "How old are you son?" "I'm twenty", I reply. He then says, "I've been doing this for longer than you've been alive, I know there's dope in that car. That's probably why your partner walked down the block. He probably went to dump the dope in the woods." His tone was now elevated and I could tell he was doing his best to intimidate me. I had never been questioned by the cops. The only cops I had ever held a conversation with was Officer Brown and Officer Brooks, the officers at our high school and that was more than likely about basketball. I felt a bit of pressure, but I was telling the truth. "Sir, I'm telling you, there is no dope in that car," I said firmly. He nods his head, shakes his finger at me and says, "Ok, we're gonna get the dogs out here and they're gonna find that dope!"

I walk back over to Spence and Dell. "They're bringing the dogs", I said. "Is there something in the car?" Spence asked. "Nah man, there's nothing in there." I replied. I wasn't the type to keep weed in the car. I bought it in small amounts, and consumed it fairly quick; so I knew the car was clean, but I wasn't sure if the cops would try to plant something in there. I was nervous. I called my dad yelling, "DAD THEY TRYNA SAY I GOT WEED IN THE CAR!" Then my phone dies, matter of fact, all our phones are dead. Six cop cars pull up, including the K-9 unit. I've always had a Love for German Shepherds, but not that night.

We stood there as the cops ripped through my car. They pulled out the back seat, took everything out of the glove box and center console, and even yanked out the lining of the trunk. The dog was jumping in and out of the car as if he was performing tricks in a dog show. After about ten minutes of searching, they realized that they weren't going to find anything. That bearable chill in the air, had now become extremely unbearable as we stood on the curb. This had been one of the worst nights of my life. My car was wrecked, my high was blown, and just when I thought it couldn't get any worse, a black Chevy Tahoe pulls up. It was Coach Preston.

Coach parks and walks over to the officers performing the search. They talk for a second and then Coach looks down the block at us. In this moment, he looked closer to 8 feet tall instead of 6'9. As he walked towards us, we wanted to be ANYWHERE but there. I guess this was how the Israelite army felt when Goliath was taunting them on the battlefield. But David wasn't showing up with his trusted slingshot that night, we were going to have to deal with whatever punishment came our way.

"Are y'all ok?" He asked. "Yes sir, we're good," we replied. I went through scenarios of how this was going to play out as we all began to walk back towards the car. I noticed all seven police cars, and all the officers on the scene. Every single one of them were white, and it seemed as though they were eager to make an arrest that night. Were we in the wrong? Yeah, for sure. But they didn't even bother to breathalyze the white girl that hit us. They gave her the ticket and sent her on her merry way. She had to have been drunk; there was no way that any sober person would have tried to make a left turn right in front of us the way she did. I could see the disappointment on the officers faces that they weren't going to be placing handcuffs on us that night. I'd heard about racism, but never experienced it. In that moment, my eyes were opened, and I never saw the world the same again.

One of the officers says to me, "the dog was hitting on three spots in your car, but we couldn't find anything." I didn't know how to respond to that, so I didn't. The lead officer pulls me aside, and says, "Make sure you stay away from guys like this. Your coach came out here to get you. Don't get caught up with these guys." I got that feeling that he thought I was the only one that played basketball because I was the tallest and I had on a Kennesaw basketball hoodie. I also felt like that was some sort of an apology for the way he approached me in the beginning of this ordeal, but I didn't have the strength to go back and forth with him. I just replied as politely as I could, "Thanks officer."

One of the members of the girls basketball team arrives and picks up Spence. She then asks, "Do y'all need a ride?" Coach responds, "No, these two are with me." Spence was done playing, so Coach no longer had a say in anything he chose to do, plus they didn't have the best relationship. Del and I got in Coach's car and didn't say a word.

The ride was silent and embarrassing. When we pulled up to the apartment, Coach finally broke the silence. "I've been in the car with you two for about five minutes now and I can smell the weed on you. What happened?" While we were standing on the curb, the three of us had come up with a story that we went to pick up Spence from a friend's house where they had been smoking and that's why the car smelled the way it did. Spence decided to take the blame for the situation because he knew that Coach couldn't say anything to him. We told Coach that story, and he told us to go upstairs and be ready for practice in the morning. I went upstairs, charged my phone, called my parents, and told them the same story. I don't think they believed it, but they didn't pry. They were just happy that I was safe. I think they knew that I was no longer they're little boy. I was growing up, and I was going to make mistakes. I was going to have to learn some hard lessons, and unfortunately, this would be one of them.

At practice the next day, Coach brought up the situation to the team. He talked about how we need to be safe and make smart decisions. He was looking at things from a parental point of view. Yes, we could have gotten a possession charge, but we could have died also. People have died in accidents that were less severe. When we finished practice, Coach pulled Del and I aside. "I know you two were scared last night." He said. "I'm glad y'all are safe. We need you to make better decisions." I knew that he was referring to Spence. I hated that we made Spence out to be the bad guy. I hated that he chose to be the sacrificial lamb in this situation, but I admired his courage. He didn't care what anyone thought about him, whether it was good or bad. I wanted that kind of confidence, but I was afraid. I was afraid of looking bad, and I was afraid of people not liking me. I thought back to my initial individual meeting with Coach Preston going into his first season as head coach. He asked me, "Breeze, what are you looking for going into this season?" No one had ever asked me that, but it didn't take long for me to come up with an answer. "I want everyone to know that I can play this game at a high level. And I want them to like me." Coach Preston quickly replied, "Not everyone is gonna like you, but they will respect you." It was one of the wisest statements I'd ever heard, but I just wasn't at that level. I felt I needed the approval of others. I had created an image that I felt I needed to live up to that was slowly draining me.

Later that day, Del, Drew and I went to the tow yard where they had taken my car. "Hey man, I'm here to get my belongings from the white Pontiac," I said to the guy at the register. "Wooo Weee! Y'all must have been in there smokin' that good stuff last night! I stuck my head in there and caught a contact high. It's out back, follow me." We laughed as we followed him to the car. The past eighteen hours had been no laughing matter, and we really needed that laugh right then.

I opened up the passenger door to get some things out of the glove box, and the first thing I notice when I looked on the floor was a nugget of weed. It wasn't much but it was something. I figured it was what Del had wasted when I pulled off after the cop spoke to us through the loudspeaker. The cops had missed it in their search last night. I called Del and Drew over, and both of them were in shock. It didn't make sense how the cops would miss this. They had flashlights, a drug dog and not to mention eyes of their own.

There was only one explanation; this had to be God protecting me. But what was He protecting me from? And why was He protecting me out of all people? I was everything that I shouldn't have been, a liar, a cheater, and a coward. And I was doing everything that I shouldn't have been doing. He was trying to get my attention, but being on the road that I was on, I missed all His signs; more like blatantly ignored them. I've learned that our relationship with our Heavenly Father, often mirrors that of our earthly fathers. There were times growing up when my dad would keep me from dangers, and there were times where he would allow me to go through certain things, so I could learn. God might have kept me from getting jammed up with the law that night, but there were some issues that needed to be worked out within me. And the only way to resolve those issues was to unfortunately learn the hard way.

Humility

"For this who exalt themselves will be humbled, and those who humble themselves will be exalted."

(Luke 14:11 NLT)

The accident was symbolic of everything that was headed my way. I was stubborn (some say I still am), prideful, and God had to humble me; and when God humbles you, it hurts.

My favorite book of The Bible is Daniel, and in chapter 4, there's a powerful king named Nebuchadnezzar. His greatness is known throughout the Earth. One night he has a dream about a tree that reaches up to the heavens for all the world to see. It had fresh green leaves, it was loaded with fruit, animals lived in its shade, and birds nested in its branches. Then one day an angel comes down from Heaven and gives orders to cut down the tree, but to leave its stump in the ground, let it be drenched with the dew of Heaven and for it to live with the animals for seven periods of time.

This dream troubled Nebuchadnezzar and he calls upon Daniel to interpret it. Daniel listens to the dream and explains to the king that the tree, represents the king himself. He has grown strong and powerful, but if he didn't turn from his wicked ways he would be removed from his kingdom and sent to live with the animals and eat grass for seven periods of time. He would live this way until he learned that God is in charge. Well, Nebuchadnezzar continued on the path that he was on and was banished from his kingdom. He lived in the fields and ate grass like a cow. The Bible goes on to say that his hair grew as long as eagle feathers and his nails were long like bird claws. He lost his mind as well.

After some time had passed, Nebuchadnezzar looked up to Heaven and his sanity returned; and in that moment, he realized that it was God who was in charge, and He puts whoever He wants in positions of authority. Ultimately Nebuchadnezzar was restored to his kingdom with even greater honor than he had before.

When I read that story two questions come to mind: Would Nebuchadnezzar have had to go through those things if he would have just changed his ways and lived righteously? And would Nebuchadnezzar have changed his ways and lived righteously if he didn't go through those things? The interesting part of that story was that Nebuchadnezzar was restored to even greater honor after he went through that humbling experience. As I reflect on this portion of my life I feel as though I was in Nebuchadnezzar's shoes. God had warned me and given me opportunities to change my ways, but I didn't take them. Now, He would have to humble me just as He did Nebuchadnezzar.

Basketball had always been my refuge, and my place of peace. When I needed answers to life's questions, often times I searched for them in the game. I found joy in basketball, and I also found success. I felt as long as long as I had the game, I would be ok. Basketball was a system that I relied on, but God has a way of showing us just how feeble these systems that we rely on truly are.

It's a gloomy Monday. Light grey clouds are covering the sky. I was walking back to my apartment from class with a couple of my teammates when my phone rings. It's Olivia. We had broken up about a week before. "Hello?" I say as I answer the phone confused as to why she's calling me. "Brandon..." she responds. I can tell that she's been crying. "What's going on?" I ask. She says something, but I can barely hear her. "I can't hear you; I'll call you when I get to the crib."

I walk in, go to my room, and call Olivia back. She answers on the first ring. "Brandon..." "Hey what's good?" I ask nonchalantly. I can hear the pools of tears filling up in her eyes as she responds, "I'm pregnant..." I've heard the expression, "my heart fell to my feet" but never understood it until then. All my strength left me as I stumbled backwards into the wall and slid down to the floor. I couldn't believe what I was hearing. I don't think I've ever been that scared in my life. "How do you know!?!" I asked. "I haven't gotten my period in a couple months, so I scheduled a doctor's appointment this morning and they confirmed it." We were both extremely young and in school. She was in a dual degree program, and I was trying to graduate and fulfill my hoop dream. Neither one of us wanted to have a child. Not now. I gained my composure and suggested that she come over a bit later so we could talk about this in person. She agreed and we hung up.

I got up off the floor and went outside to the balcony. By now, those light grey clouds have grown dark. I sit down and it starts to rain. I look up in the clouds and give a half-suppressed laugh. "How fitting" I think to myself.

The first person I called was my sister, Tia. "Hey B-Rad!" She called me that because of the movie Malibu's Most Wanted. "T, I need to speak with you. You at the house?" She knew something was up, "Yeah, come on by."

When I got there, I told Tia everything. She asked the first question that any Loving sister should ask when her little brother comes to her with a situation like this, "Are you sure it's yours?" I wanted to laugh, but the situation was just too heavy. "Yeah, I'm sure it's mine. I've been a bit reckless" I responded.

Tia listened as I talked the situation out. I told her how I was afraid of what my parents would say. The moment of my dad dropping me off at school, giving me a box of condoms and saying "don't bring no babies home" was on a loop in my head; and I could only imagine all the tears that my Mom would be crying. I also told her how I was afraid that my life would change. Basketball would be over for sure.

After a while, I got a call from Olivia saying that she was on her way to the apartment. It was time for me to go. During the conversation Tia kept encouraging me, "It's all gonna be alright Brandon. Trust me, it's not the end of the world." It sure felt like it though. I left Tia's place feeling a bit more hopeful. Sometimes all you need is for someone to listen and some encouragement.

I pulled up to the apartment about ten minutes before Olivia arrived. She knocked at the door with eyes filled with tears, although the rain had hidden most of them. We went into my room and she fell into my arms. I had seen a range of emotions from her. I'd seen anger. I had also seen disappointment, but never this. She was truly afraid, and so was I. But this was no time for us to stew in our emotions. We had some decisions to make. "What do you wanna do?" I asked. "I can't have a kid right now" she replied. "Neither can I." There wasn't much more to talk about after that. We found an abortion clinic in Atlanta and set an appointment for the following week.

A few days later I received a text message from Olivia. It was a picture. She was holding a small photograph in her hand. It was an ultrasound, and I could see the head of a baby being formed. I had been with girls who've had pregnancy scares, but this was not a drill; this was the real thing. This woman was carrying my child. The days leading up to the abortion were the most stressful days that I've ever lived through. We had two games that week, one against Mercer University in Macon, Ga, and the other against The University of North Florida at home in Kennesaw. I did my best to block out all my off the court issues and focus on basketball, but I would find that to be impossible. During the Mercer game I drove to the hoop and made a difficult layup over a defender that was 6'10 while being fouled. But when I stepped to the free throw line to complete the three-point play, the thought of me being a father flashed through my mind and I missed the free throw. It was downhill from there.

Against North Florida, I played horrible from the very beginning. Missed shot, turnover, bad defensive rotation, blown assignment. It was one bad play after another all night. Towards the end game I got subbed out and as I'm walking to the bench, I untuck my jersey and say "F*** this s***" and take a seat. After the game I get a text from Coach Preston. "Meet me in my office at 8am tomorrow" it read. "Great, what have I done now?" I thought. The next morning, I walk in, and I can tell Coach is frustrated (we've been losing games all year, I'd be frustrated too). We skipped all the pleasantries and he just flat out asked me, "Did you untuck your jersey and say f*** this s*** when you got to the bench last night?" I figured one of the assistant coaches had told him what I said. See, the problem wasn't that I was cursing; the problem was he thought that I was disrespecting the team and the coaching staff. He thought that I wasn't all in.

But my disgruntled behavior had nothing to do with him or the team, it was all due to my personal life, and unfortunately, I didn't trust Coach enough to have those kinds of conversations with him. So, I lied. "No sir." I said with a confused look on my face. "I said f***, I'm playing like s***." (I was a decent liar in those days). I couldn't tell if he bought it or not, but I left the office knowing that he wasn't happy with me. Normally basketball brought me peace, but right now it felt like a burden.

During this time, Olivia's mother had come across the ultrasound photo in her room and confronted her about it. "Do Brandon's parents know about this?" her mother asked. Knowing that her parents would want to speak with my parents, she covered for me, "It's not Brandon's." When she told me that, I realized how down for me she really was. She made herself look bad in front of her parents just to keep my secret safe. I thought that was extremely noble, and I knew that I didn't deserve her sacrifice.

One of Olivia's friends drove her to the appointment. I was nervous the entire day because I didn't know exactly how everything would turn out. I was told that there was a large group of people protesting outside the clinic, and I didn't know if Olivia would be able to go through with it. I feared that I would get out of practice and get a message from her that said something like, "I couldn't do it." I was afraid that my life would change, and all my dreams and aspirations of becoming a professional basketball player would be dismantled before my very eyes. If that were the case, it would be no one's fault but my own.

I got a message from Olivia later that day saying that everything was finished and that she was at home resting. I felt relieved that it was finally over. We had a game that weekend, and I was able to play with a clear mind. That made a big difference.

A few days later, I was with some teammates watching our women's team play. I saw Selena at the gym, the one who asked me if the weed was too strong that night I passed out at her place. She and some of her friends came over and watched the game with us. We had a few laughs and she says, " Yo, I gotta tell you something…" Whenever someone tells me that I'm on edge because it's usually information that I don't want or need to know. "What's up?" I said as I braced myself for impact. "I f***** yo b****, n****!" She said in a joking manner. "What???" I was extremely confused. She went on to tell me that her and Olivia had messed around one night after a few drinks. Yep, just like I thought, this was information that I didn't need or want to know. I couldn't believe what I was hearing. Selena and I had been cool since high school; she was a year younger than me, but we had gotten really close my senior year. She was like a little sister to me. In my mind, it was just as bad as Olivia having sex with another guy. Even though I had cheated on Olivia quite a few times, I felt betrayed, not only by Olivia, but by Selena.

I called Olivia while I was at the game and confronted her about the situation. She was surprised that I knew, but also surprised that it bothered me. "It's not like I was with another guy, why does that matter?" she said. She met me at Selena's apartment and all three of us tried to talk it out, but there was nothing that they could say that would make me change my stance on the situation.

I yelled, I cursed. Finally, Selena says, "Brandon! What are you doing? Why are you acting like that? This b**** just had an abortion and you in here yelling at her about some old sh** that doesn't really matter." In that moment, something clicked within me. I realized that I had been so selfish throughout the entire ordeal that I hadn't even checked on Olivia during this process. I was only concerned about my future and what I had going on. Even though Olivia and I weren't together anymore, I still should have been there for her. Deep down, I knew she had the abortion because I wasn't man enough to raise a kid back then. She had always talked about how she wanted to be a mother someday to a little girl. That was her opportunity, but she gave it up for me. Plus, I had cheated on Olivia more times than I could count, I really had no right to be mad. I wasn't mature enough to apologize. I looked at them, got in my car and left. After that, my relationship with Selena slowly began to deteriorate. We would only talk to each other a few more times.

Forward

"Look straight ahead, and fix your eyes on what lies before you."
(Proverbs 4:25 NLT)

After the abortion, it seemed like my life fell apart. Coach Preston and I weren't seeing eye to eye; I felt that I deserved more of an opportunity on the court, but he didn't see it that way. My grades started to fall; I went from having a 3.0 GPA to a 2.3. And that calm and patient person that I once was, didn't exist anymore.

Olivia and I were trying to work things out and went to Downtown Atlanta one Sunday to hang and get something to eat. I had just finished smoking with one of my teammates when I got into her car. My eyes red, low, and I had that stupid grin on my face that I would get whenever I was high. She looked at me concerned and said, "You've been smoking a lot lately. Are you ok?" I looked at her, sucked my teeth and replied, "Yeah, I'm cool." But I wasn't cool. I realized that all the difficulties I was facing was due to my poor decision making, but I didn't have the courage to take responsibility for it; So, I blamed it on everyone else. It was everyone's fault but my own.

I was sitting at my desk one day when I got a call from Coach Roth. Coach Roth was on the coaching staff at Kennesaw when I first arrived my freshman year. He was a great guy, extremely passionate, and always willing to get in the gym and help you put in some extra work. "Breeze, what's up man!" he said as I answered the phone. We talked for a few minutes, and he went on to tell me that he had been keeping up with the situation over at Kennesaw and there were a lot of coaches asking about me. "I've had quite a few coaches call about you. They see what's going on over there. They want to know if you're interested in transferring."

Kennesaw was home, and I had never thought about transferring, but at this point I wasn't opposed to the idea. I didn't see things getting any better for me there. Coach Preston and I were at odds, and I doubted we'd be on the same page anytime soon. I saw this scenario playing out one of two ways: Either I was going to be buried on the bench, or he was going to cut me. It was clear to see that I was effective when I was on the floor, but I felt like something else was going on; something behind the scenes that I had no control over and was affecting my playing time. I couldn't put my finger on it, and ultimately chalked it up to Coach Preston just not being a fan of mine.

One of the coaches that was interested in me was Mike Leeder over at Georgia Southwestern University, a division 2 school in Americus, Ga, about four hours from Kennesaw. Coach Roth told me that he wanted to meet with me if I had some time soon. Spring Break was coming up the following week and we decided to meet at the Hooters on Peachtree Street in Atlanta. When I met with Coach Leeder, he spoke to me about where I could fit in with his program. He had watched me on film and was impressed by my versatility. I still wasn't 100% sure about transferring, but it felt good to hear someone compliment my game. After going through that last season at Kennesaw my confidence was completely shot. I told him that this was a big decision for me, and I still needed some time to think about transferring. He understood.

A couple weeks went by, and workouts resumed at Kennesaw. I

could tell by the way Coach Preston is running the workouts that he's feeling the pressure. That cool, calm, and approachable demeanor that he had when he first arrived was gone, and now a lot of us felt like we weren't even able to hold a conversation with him. As a head coach, he had back-to-back three-win seasons, so I understood. It was make or break time or him. At this point, he was at a place of not wanting to hear excuses, he just wanted results; But it almost came from a place where it seemed like he didn't care for us. When I say us, I'm referring to Drew and myself. We were now the only players left from the Ingle regime, and it felt as though he had some animosity towards us. My loyalty was one of my greatest attributes and my biggest flaws. When I say I'm in, I'm in, whether we win or lose. But one person can only take so much.

It was a Friday, and we were finishing up workouts for the week. Fridays were the hardest days because we started having these Olympic type workouts on the track. They were tough, and borderline barbaric. Once, we had to wrestle each other for a mop handle. Both participants started with two hands on the handle and whoever was able to take it from the other person was declared the winner. I think Coach liked this because it forced us to compete. Competing was big for him. He stressed how important it was to be a competitor day in and day out. One day I pinned a teammate under my foot and almost forced the end of the handle into his face in order to take it from him. All I heard was my teammates yell out, "BREEZE NO!" as I stood over him. It looked like a scene out of that movie 300.

But this Friday, Coach had us carrying each other around the track. We were divided up into groups of three. My group consisted of Del and Drew. Del was about 6'0 tall and weighed around 185lbs.

Drew was 6'9 and weighed 270lbs. Del wasn't hard for Drew and I to carry but Drew was extremely hard for me and Del to carry. Drew had to decided not to hold himself up either, so it was like we were carrying dead weight. This was torture. I fell to my knees and held my back as it starts to spaz out. Del was hunched over on his knees, and Drew was gasping for air from the previous drill.

Coach Preston yells from the starting pointing of the track, "Breeze, get your a** up!" like I was the only one struggling. That was the straw that broke the camel's back. I said to myself, "This is bull****." I didn't see how us carrying each other around a track would help us with basketball. Maybe Coach was looking for some kind of intrinsic Rocky Balboa inspiration to hit us about being able to help elevate our teammates or something; I'm not sure. All I knew was that this wasn't working for me. I was tired of playing behind people who I knew I should have been playing in front of. I was tired of walking on eggshells because I wasn't sure if my coach liked me. I was tired of trying to win the approval of everyone else. At that moment, I knew that my time at Kennesaw was up.

The following Monday, we had workouts scheduled for 8am. I texted Coach Preston around 7:30am asking if I could come and speak with him. "Good morning, we can talk after workouts" he replied. "What I have to talk to you about is my continuation in the program" I responded. "Come see me at 2:30pm. I'll be in my office."

I show up to his office at 2:20pm, and I can feel the tension in the air. By this time, everyone knows what this conversation could possibly entail, and I'm public enemy #1. I've never made a decision this big; I'm nervous, but I'm ready. I'm constantly checking my phone, minutes feel like hours. 2:24pm, 2:25pm, 2:26pm… 2:28pm. The door opens and Coach Lallathin steps out. I hear Coach Preston ask, "Is Breeze out there?" "Yeah" Coach Lallathin replies. "Tell him to come on in." Coach Lallathin gives me the head nod signaling me to enter. As he holds the door open for me, he refuses to make eye contact, letting me know that he already knows what's about to go down.

"What's on your mind Breeze?" Coach Preston asks as I walk in. He points to the couch as he takes a seat in the adjacent chair. As I sit down, I take my Adidas backpack off and set it on the floor a lot harder than I intended to. Yep, definitely nervous. "Well, after a lot of prayer (which was a lie because I was not praying in those days) I've decided that it's best that I transfer." Coach Preston folds one of his legs over the other and then puts on a face that suggests he's in deep thought. "What makes you feel that way?" He asks. "Honestly coach, I just don't think you're going to give me a fair opportunity." "So, you're afraid to compete!" he retorts (Told you he was big on competing). I give my famous half suppressed laugh and by this time the nerves are gone. I reply "no, it's not that. I just don't feel that this is the place for me anymore." Nodding his head he says, "Ok, I understand. I respect your decision. It's been a pleasure." We stand and shake hands. The fact that he didn't say that he wanted me to stay, confirmed that he thought it was best that I leave too. I walked out of the office KNOWING that I made the right decision.

A Word from God

"Thy word is a lamp unto my feet, And a light unto my path."
(Psalm 119:105 KJV)

The semester ended, and so did my time at Kennesaw. It was harder than I thought to leave. Even though I had a lot of issues, and my experience was nothing like I hoped it would be, I still had a lot of Love for Kennesaw State University. I still do. I packed up my car and said my goodbyes. It felt like the last episode of The Fresh Prince of Bel-Air, or Martin. I didn't want to say goodbye, but I just knew it was time. I had reached the end. It was time to go back to Tucker and figure out where I would be going to school in the fall.

The next day I went to a conference in Woodstock, GA with my mom. Bishop John Paul Jackson was speaking. My mom Loved to watch him preach on TV about dreams and visions from God and their true meaning. I had seen him a few times, but I didn't know much about him. Honestly, I didn't really care to go, but my mom asked if I would accompany her a few weeks prior, so I agreed to come.

It was a Saturday morning and we got there around 9am. It wasn't a huge conference, there might have only been about thirty-five people there. It was held in the upper room of an older brick building in downtown Woodstock. I had been in settings like this before, and I expected it to be like all the others. You come in, sing, pray, hear a word from the speaker, and go home. But this time, things were different. This time I wouldn't leave the same way I came in.

Bishop John Paul Jackson came out and spoke for about an hour or so, and then released us for lunch. They had sandwiches, drinks, and chips for us to choose from. But just before he dismisses us, he points into the crowd and says, "You, stand up." Everyone turns their heads, and all eyes are on me. The room is quiet, and I point to myself and say, "me?" "Yes, you!" he replies. I was nervous. I'd seen things like this before where the preacher gets a word from God and starts to call out all the sins you've been partaking in. If this was that, I wouldn't mind, but I just hated that it would be in front of my mom. She didn't need to hear about all that.

Bishop John Paul Jackson then asked, "Is that your wife sitting next to you?" I look to my right. "That's my mom," I reply. The crowd laughs and so does he. He goes on to say, "The enemy (devil) has tried to kill you three times when you were a child." As a child, my mom would often tell me about how I almost died when I was in the womb and when I was a baby when I came down with pneumonia. The third time was when I tried to commit suicide and ended up in the hospital in the 8th grade. This information about me was never publicized and I knew then that this man was hearing CLEARLY from God. I began to listen more intently as he spoke.

"You're an athlete, and God has frustrated your game. You thought that it was the enemy that was doing this, but it was God. He has called you to be a 'leader of leaders' and you're going to do some mighty things for His Kingdom."

At this point my mom is in tears because she knows that all of this is true. Since I was a young boy, mom has always told me that I would be a preacher, but that wasn't what I wanted for my life, so I rejected the idea. Matter of fact, I ran from it. This was just confirmation of the things God had told her about me long ago.

I thanked Bishop John Paul Jackson and took my seat. "A leader of leaders?" I thought to myself. I didn't know how to be that, nor was it something that I wanted to do. I wanted to ask him, "where does basketball fit in with God's plan for my life?" But I didn't. Everything he said sounded good and I knew it had to be from God; but all I wanted to do was play ball. I wasn't ready to live out God's plan. I was still trying to establish plans of my own.

I had it in my mind that I would live out God's plan when I was done playing basketball. Like so many people, I put my plans first. To be honest, I wanted God's plan to line up with the plans that I had for myself. Since I was a child, all I knew is that I wanted to play basketball, and this was the first time in a long time that I had been away from the game. I felt that my days with the game I had fallen so deeply in Love with were numbered.

For the rest of the conference people kept coming up and congratulating me like I had won the lottery or something. I thought it was cool that God had plans for me to be a "leader of leaders", but it felt like my dreams and desires would be assassinated in the process. I wasn't ready for that. I think lots of people have an idea of what God's plans for their lives are, but they feel if they submit to His plans, they're killing their dreams.

That summer I had schools from all over the country calling me and wanting me to come and visit, but I only went to visit five: Tarleton State (Texas), Virginia State (Virginia), Young Harris (Georgia), Clayton State (Georgia) and Columbus State (Georgia). All of them were good schools, and I could see myself finishing up my collegiate career at either one of them, but I didn't know which one to choose. I was afraid to make the wrong decision. I was getting on the plane, heading back to Atlanta from my tour of Virginia State. I sat down next to a guy, and he immediately began to ask me questions. I'm sure you've been next to those kind of people on planes. "Hi, how are you? What do you do?" he asked. What I wanted to say was, "Well, I'm a college student-athlete whose life is in absolute shambles right now, and I just want to get on this plane and go to sleep." But I played it cool, "I'm a college-student athlete. I'm transferring schools and I came up here to visit one of the schools that's been recruiting me."

We talked for a few minutes, and I can't remember exactly what he said, but it was something along the lines of, "You know what school to go to. Go to the one that brings you the most peace." Immediately, it was like the fog had been lifted from my mind, and my thoughts were clear. His statement was so simple, yet it brought me so much clarity. I got back home and told my parents that I would be going to Columbus State in the fall.

My man, Nick Turner, had transferred to Columbus State and had been doing well down there. He'd been telling me about the school, and I enjoyed my visit. I remembered our conversation in his apartment when I was there, "Man, if you come here, it'll be just like old times. Up late playing NBA 2K, hanging out, going to the gym whenever we want. Plus, we have a good team. We'll win more than three games. But this is a big decision, you've gotta make sure it's right for you." He was right, this was a big decision. People don't get a second chance to make a decision like this, most people don't even get a chance to make a decision like this once. But I felt that Columbus was right for me, and when I told him that I'd be joining him, he was ecstatic, and so was I.

I had gotten a job that summer working at United Distributors, a liquor distributor in Smyrna, GA. This was my first job, and my first time filling out a job application. I didn't know what position I was applying for so when I was filling out the application and it asked me "position applying for" I put "whatever's available." I still cringe when I think about that. Nick and I both had uncle's that worked there, and they helped just get us the jobs. Nick had worked there the summer he left Kennesaw and then later told me about it. We never worked there at the same time though. I had to be there Monday – Friday starting at 5am. It was twenty-five miles from my parents' house in Stone Mountain. I would wake up at 4am, and leave the house at 4:15, and get there by 4:45. I worked there for almost two months, and I was never late. My job was simple. I would be riding in the box trucks and helping deliver wine/liquor to various locations throughout Georgia. We mainly delivered in Atlanta but my first day was right before 4th of July and I found myself making deliveries in Tennessee. I think I worked about fifteen hours that day.

For the most part, I liked it. It was difficult lifting those cases of liquor in the hot sun and hauling them in and out of gas stations, package stores, and restaurants, but I got to meet some cool people and see parts of the city that I might not have ever seen. A lot of the guys who I rode with were fifteen to twenty years older than me and were able to give me a lot of knowledge about life. They told me about their mistakes and things they struggled with and warned me not to go down the same paths. I appreciated that. At this point in my life, I was willing to learn from anyone that I came across. It didn't matter what your occupation was, or how old you were, I just wanted to learn. Although I couldn't admit it, I realized that my pride had knocked me off the pedestal that I so arrogantly placed myself on. I had gotten caught up with the women, and the lifestyle that I was living, and I didn't abide by the number one rule that my dad had preached to me as a kid; I forgot to handle my business.

We didn't just deliver to restaurants, gas stations, and package stores. We delivered to strip clubs too. I had been to a couple strip clubs before, but they weren't really my thing. It was…weird… seeing people in the strip club at 10am. I always thought going to the strip club was more of an evening outing. One day, as we were delivering to a strip club in stone Mountain, I saw a famous rapper and an NBA player shooting a music video around 12pm. They were throwing money into a large fan which was blowing the money back at them, and there were a few girls dancing behind them. When you watch a video like that on TV it seems like a lot is going on, but when you're watching it in person, it's very anticlimactic. The cinematography makes it seem more exciting than what it really is.

I learned a lot about Atlanta and life from working that job, and I Loved that; but the downside was that it was so physically demanding that I didn't have the energy or time to really work out and my game suffered because of it. Mentally, I was ready for this new start though. Columbus was about two hours away from Atlanta and this would be the furthest I've ever been away from home for an extended period of time. Having Nick down there with me helped ease my mind though. Nick, Olivia, and I left for Columbus on a Saturday afternoon. We followed each other in a convoy. Each of them carrying some of my belongings that I would need at my new school. I told my parents that they didn't need to worry about helping me get moved in. I had been in college before, and them making that two-hour drive would just be a waste of their time. I knew what I had to do.

I've always enjoyed driving. It's always been such a freeing experience, especially on an open road like I-185 from Atlanta to Columbus. During this drive, I took time to meditate on what I needed to do at my new school. One of my teammates from Kennesaw, Kelvin McConnell, looked me in my eyes and told me, "handle your business when you get to your new school." I think that was his way of telling me that I was wasting my potential and I needed to get myself together. His words were plastered in my mind as I switched lanes and sped up to keep up with Nick and Olivia.

I no longer had time for games. I wasn't looking to play around and party down here. I just wanted to play basketball, graduate, and get out of there. Honestly, I felt some shame about going to Columbus. I felt like the narrative was that I was one of those players who couldn't cut it. I felt like I had fallen by the wayside, like I was damaged goods in a way; which was part of the reason I told my parents not to worry about helping me move in.

That two-hour drive seemed to take forever and a day. Maybe it was because I didn't know exactly what to expect, or maybe it was because I was afraid of failing again. I wasn't sure. Just then our convoy came up on three Kennesaw State University campus buses. We must have been no more than half an hour from our destination. It didn't make any sense that those buses were that far from Kennesaw; And at that moment, I knew in my heart that I wasn't finished there. I didn't have any doubt that I was on the right path, and I was sure that I had made the right decision to leave. But I somehow knew that my path would lead me back to Kennesaw someday.

Wilderness

"Then the devil went away, and angels came and took care of Jesus."
(Matthew 4:11 NLT)

My mindset going into Columbus was completely different than it was going into Kennesaw. I no longer wanted to be the center of attention, nor did I look to prove anything to anyone. I felt as though I had let so many people down because of the way things played out at KSU, including myself. I didn't care to be the ladies' man anymore, and I didn't care if people thought I was cool or not. Giving attention to what people thought of me was the reason I went through so much drama at my last school. I saw Columbus as my shot at redemption.

My coaches quickly saw the talent I possessed and made me one of the team captains. Honestly, it wasn't a role that I was looking to be in. Being a team captain meant that I had to be more of a vocal leader, and that wasn't my style. I was more of the "lead by example" type. I'd rather show you, than tell you. I had spurts of greatness, especially at the beginning of the season. I thought that I was going to finally have the success that I was capable of having, but my struggles with consistency continued. Before long, I found myself buried on the bench; and the fire that once burned so brightly was now flickering like a flame in adverse winds and on the brink of burning out. I would come home from practices and games and lock myself in my room and just cry. I began to regret my decision to leave Kennesaw and I often wondered, "what if I would have stayed?" Would my situation have gotten any better? Or would I still be fighting a losing battle against the coaching staff? I realized that no matter what decision you make in life, whether it be good or bad, you're always going to be left wondering, "what if?"

When I initially left Kennesaw, it was to fulfill my own selfish desires. I wanted to show everyone that I didn't need their help and that I could accomplish my goals on my own. But that wasn't God's intent. This was God's way of humbling me and bringing me back to Him; and in order to do so He had to eliminate all my distractions. That included removing me from, Kennesaw, the very place He called me to be.

Whether we like it or not, we all must go through a wilderness of some sort. Jesus went through the wilderness and was attacked by satan. He thought during this time Jesus would be weak and not able to withstand his temptations (Matthew 4:1-11). But what he didn't realize was although many people die in the wilderness, it strengthens others. I saw that the troubles that I faced at Kennesaw and what I was now going through in Columbus, was my wilderness. Whether I lived or died was up to me.

In the eleventh verse of Matthew, chapter four, when Jesus had withstood the temptation of satan, it says something that has always been interesting to me, "Then the devil went away, and angels came and took care of Jesus." It doesn't say who these angels were, or how many came. All it says is they came and took care of Jesus. Though I tried to hide it, it was clear to see that I was in a vulnerable state while I was in Columbus. God, and bad decision making on my part, had broken me all the way down; but God isn't the type to break things down and not rebuild them. He surrounded me with three guys who would serve as the angels that would help me during my time in the wilderness: Nick, Bejay, and Chris.

Bejay was me and Nick's roommate and was a year younger than us. He had transferred from a school in North Carolina although Orlando, FL was home for him. He was going into his junior year at Columbus. One of the things that stood out about Bejay was how things always seemed to come so easy to him. He would knock down deep three pointers with just the flick of his wrist. He would go up and dunk on defenders and it looked like he wasn't even going hard. This ease also spilled over into his personal life. He handled stressful situations with a smile and grace. He was always cool, and always under control, no matter the circumstance. People that know me would argue that I possessed the same qualities. The difference was, mine was just covering up the scared and insecure young man that I really was, while his were genuine.

Chris was the manager for the basketball team. I remember seeing him at conditioning one day and the first thing I noticed about him was his shoes. He was wearing the black and purple Adidas Top ten 2000's. Most of my teammates wore Nike's and Jordan's and when I saw him, I walked up and said, "finally someone with some culture around here." Chris was a Columbus native and always giving us a history lesson about the city. What impressed me the most about Chris was the way he carried himself. Much like Bejay, he was always under control. Even when situations got a little sticky, he was able to keep his composure. He was a professional. He was also a couple years older than Nick, Bejay, and I and had a job working with Parks and Rec for the city of Columbus. Since he was a bit older, he had accomplished some things that the three of us hadn't yet. He had bought a car, he had his own apartment, which was right below ours; and he paid his own bills. I was astonished that he was only a couple years older than me but carried himself like a grown man, while I still felt like a kid. Being friends with Chris was like taking a master class in adulthood; he often showed us what to do and what not to do.

Sitting on the bench and not playing as much as I thought I should was taking a toll on me, but being around Nick, Bejay, and Chris made me think there could be more to life than just basketball. We hung out every day and soon the pain from not playing, didn't hurt as much. I didn't come home from practice and games and cry in my room anymore; and I realized that being around good people is good for you. I saw how foolish it was for me to think that I didn't need people in my life. In the New Testament, one of the religious leaders asked Jesus, "what is the most important commandment?" Jesus replied, "You must Love God with all your heart, all your soul, and all your mind. This is the first and greatest commandment. A second is equally important: Love your neighbor as you Love yourself." (Matthew 22:37-40) He went on to say that all the commandments are based on these two commands. To sum it up, Love God and Love people. I saw that we were created to be in relationship with one another. Matter of fact, the reason God made Eve was because He looked upon Adam and said, "It's not good for man to be alone (Genesis 2:18)." Through my relationship with Nick, Bejay, and Chris, I was learning how to truly Love the people that God had placed in my life. Next was to learn how to truly Love God.

Salvation

"If you Love me, obey my commandments."
(John 14:15 NLT)

I remember being at a Bible study one night at Kennesaw. It was called "925 Ministries" which was a ministry that was held once a week on campus for student-athletes. I felt obligated to go in order to show God that I was trying. I also wanted to be able to tell my mom that I was going to Bible study. She was worried about me and the things I was doing and knowing that I was going to bible study would ease her mind. Plus, it was right across the street from our apartment in the baseball complex, so I had no excuse to not show up. A few of my teammates would often come too. This particular night, the minister had an altar call for people who wanted to rededicate their lives to Christ or give their lives to Christ for the first time. About 90% of the students stood up proclaiming that they wanted to make a change in their lives; I was among that 90%. My teammates and I noticed that Del didn't stand though, so we asked him why when we got back to the apartment. "You too good to stand up for God, Del!?" one of my teammates joked. "Ya'll really gonna tell me that all of ya'll are about to stop doing the stuff that ya'll do!?" he replied. The room went silent. "Breeze, you probably about to sleep with a girl tonight," he said. He was right. I had literally just finished setting up a late-night rendezvous. He went on to say, "all ya'll looked like hypocrites in there tonight." Del was telling the truth; none of us were truly willing to turn from our ways and follow God. We just wanted it to look like we would. We were all hypocrites, and that conversation stuck with me for a long time.

Now that I was at Columbus, I wasn't sure which direction my life was going. I wanted to turn away from all the things that held me back, but I felt like I had done too much, and that God didn't want to hear from me. There were so many times where I would do things that I knew I had no business doing, only to ask Him for forgiveness, but then turn around and do the same thing again. Keeping God's word appeared too difficult, and I didn't see a way out of the cycle of sin that had entrapped me.

Nick gave me a book one day entitled "Paradise" by Mark Cahill. "This is one of my dad's teammates from Auburn. He's an evangelist now and I think you might like this," he said as he leaned against the frame of my bedroom door. I jumped off the bed and took a look. The cover was captivating, showing a picture of a beautiful beach sunset. Nick had given me one of his books before during our freshman year at Kennesaw, but I never got around to reading it, so it was my mission to read this one. "Thanks! I'm definitely gonna check this out," I replied.

A few days later we were heading to South Carolina to play Lander University, which was about a four-hour ride from Columbus. As I packed my bag the night before we left, I saw "Paradise" sitting on my desk. "I'll bring this to read on the way," I thought. I enjoyed reading, but I didn't read as much because I thought that basketball players had to be all about…basketball. It didn't seem like there was time for books to be honest. So, I never made time to read. I guess I was living up to a stereotype.

The charter bus was packed. The men's and women's teams often times traveled together to save money which was a big difference from Kennesaw. The women's team was at the front and the men's team sat in the back, while all the coaches sat in the first few seats by the door. I never liked to sit all the way in the back because it was always too noisy, so Nick and I found some seats towards the middle.

As soon as we hit the interstate, I pulled out Paradise. I didn't know what it was, but I felt as though I was supposed to be reading that book at that time, because I read all 221 pages in about three hours. I had never read anything that fast. Up to that point, I think I had only read a handful of books completely, and most of them were by Dr. Seuss. I don't want to tell you the whole story, so I'll give you a quick synopsis. It was a about a guy who went on vacation with his family and some friends from college. While there, people are telling him that he needs to give his life to Christ. He wants to, but there is something holding him back. There are so many signs around him that are telling him it's time to give your life to Christ, but he makes the mistake that so many of us often do… He thinks that he has time.

"Time is a luxury that we can't afford. Not even the richest man can get it back." That was a quote that I had heard plenty of times throughout my life, but I didn't really understand the meaning until after I read Paradise. I thought to myself, "What if I die right now? What if we get in an accident and everyone on this bus dies?" Some might say I was trippin', but I've seen stories where a bus full of student athletes were going to play somewhere and they get in an accident, and everyone dies. This was a real-life situation and I had to ask myself, "If I were to die right now, where would I go? Heaven or Hell?"

I sat for a second and thought about all the things that I had done in my life, but mainly the events that had taken place over the past three years. I thought about the lies, the cheating, the countless sexual partners. I thought about the horrible ways that I made people feel. I thought about how my parents would be disappointed if they only knew about some of the things that I was out there doing. I thought about the abortion. But more importantly, I thought about how God was probably disappointed in me too. I knew that I could no longer go on like that, and it was time to make a change. I was broken and I realized that I didn't know how to fix myself. Basketball, sex, weed, and alcohol were only temporary fixes. I needed something that was going to be permanent. I needed something that would last for this lifetime and the next.

I had searched for myself on basketball courts all across America, in swisher sweets and bags of the funkiest weed, and in the beds of women who were lost and searching for something as well. I was out of options, and places to look. Tears began to form in my eyes as I bowed my head, and with a heavy heart I whispered a simple prayer. "Lord, If I were to die right now, I want to be with You. Please forgive me." I've said prayers like this before, but this time was different; this time I meant it. IMMEDIATELY I could feel a change happening inside of me, and a peace befell me that was so immense, it felt like I could reach out and touch it.

People tend to think that when you give your life to Christ, that you have to walk down an aisle in a church and make the confession in front of a congregation. In Western society that's how it's typically portrayed, but that's not how it always has to be. See, Jesus doesn't care where you are. I've heard stories of people giving their lives to Christ in bathrooms, restaurants, offices, etc. Salvation had come to me on a bus going to play a basketball game (Where I had one of the most interesting dunks of my career by the way). Jesus doesn't care where you are… He just wants you.

Another misconception that people have is that when you give your life to Christ, everything just magically gets better. It doesn't. In fact, this is where the real work begins. All throughout The Bible it tells us to "seek God", and to seek means to actively pursue or go after. Many people just sit around and wait. If there was one thing that basketball had taught me, it was that nothing comes to the person who just waits. If I was on the court and I just stood in the corner and waited for someone to pass me the ball, they probably weren't going to pass it to me. But if I wanted the ball, I had to put myself in position to get it. I figured God was the same way. If I wanted Him, I was going to have to put myself in position to get Him.

I made a habit of reading The Bible and listening to sermons every day; and I slowly began to notice that my desire to spend time with God was starting to outweigh my desire to go out and do things that didn't honor Him. The more time I spent with God, the more clarity I began to see in my life. Situations that once stressed me out, were no longer able to disrupt the peace that I now had. I even felt lighter. It was almost as if I had taken off a weighted vest, and now walked around completely unhindered. I was in a rhythm with God which was almost like being in the zone in basketball. During that time, I felt like I could do no wrong, and I made every shot that I put up. But in basketball, if you're in a rhythm, the defense is going to do everything they can to disrupt it. Our enemy, satan, is the same way.

It was our senior night game. I played the first two minutes and sat on the bench for the remaining thirty-eight. I was so angry because I knew that I was better than two minutes worth of playing time. To make matters worse, my parents and my brother Josh had drove two hours just to watch me sit on the bench. I was embarrassed and I wished that they wouldn't have wasted their time. I couldn't wait for the game to be over. All I wanted to do that night was smoke, drink, and party. I felt like that was the only way to express how I was feeling.

That night Olivia and I got into an argument about me going to a party. She didn't like when I went to parties because there were other women there. At this point I had been in Columbus for a few months, and I hadn't gone to many parties simply because I knew how she felt and I knew she didn't trust me; but tonight, I needed to get out and clear my mind. She was having a hard time understanding that, or maybe I was having a hard time communicating how I felt. My pride wouldn't allow me to tell her that I was hurting because I sat on the bench all game in front of my family. I couldn't tell her that there was a void in me from not achieving the way I thought I was capable of in college. All I could say was, "leave me alone, I'm going out", as I hung up the phone. She had every right to feel the way she did. I had put her through so much with my escapades with other women during my time in Kennesaw, but my pride had me thinking she was trying to control me. And the thought of being controlled was a trigger. I felt like I had been controlled my entire life by coaches and my parents, and it was time to start making some decisions of my own.

There was this girl who I would often see around campus. She was a very petite girl, and I would always catch her giving me seductive looks, but I never made a move. We even shared a math class together and I often caught her flirting with me from across the room. She had even gone as far as to tell some of my teammates that she liked me, but I paid it no mind. I had a girlfriend, and I was trying to get closer to God. I wasn't interested in going back to the life I was living, but tonight was different. I knew that she would be at this party, and I went there to find her.

The party was at this house not too far from downtown Columbus. I walked in, greeted some of my teammates and went to get a drink. I saw the girl in my peripheral, and I made sure to pass by her on my way to the refreshments. She noticed me, and I noticed her. I played it cool, while drinking my drink and contemplating if I was really going to go through with this. A part of me was telling me that it wasn't worth it, while the other part was telling me I had nothing to lose.

A few moments later, the girl and I make eye contact. I signal for her to step into the backyard of the house with me. As I sit on the air conditioning unit, she stands in front of me. She crosses her legs and begins to sway side to side while playing with her hair. I sit back and continue to sip my drink. We smile at one another, then I take another sip of the brown liquor while taking in some of the ice that cooled the beverage. I let out that famous half-suppressed laugh and said, "So, whats up, you gon stop playin?" She sucks her teeth and replies, "You the one playin…" implying that she's been trying to get with me, but I haven't made any moves. She was right, I was playing. I smirk, adjust my hat, and raise my left eyebrow. She moves in closer; I place my hands on her waist and she kisses me. I look around, and I see that a few people are making their way into the backyard. "Let's leave" I propose. "I'm following you" she replies as she sends a text message to her homegirls to let them know that she had a ride.

    We had sex that night, and usually after sex, I felt a sense of accomplishment. I felt as though I was fulfilling my duty as a man, I felt like I was embracing who I truly was. I had cheated before, and to be honest, it was never about the other woman; it was always about the thrill. It was exhilarating, and it was fun. But not this time; this time, all I felt was shame. The burden was so heavy that I didn't even want to leave my apartment the next day. There was something inside of me telling me that I was wrong, and honestly, that scared me. I knew it was God. I think part of the reason I had gone through with it was because I feared change, and I didn't think I had it in me to become who God wanted me to be. I went to the girl after math class the following Monday and explained to her that I couldn't do that again, and I apologized for even putting her in that position. She was disappointed because as she was leaving the other night, we had discussed making this a regular thing, but I couldn't go through with it. There had been so many times where I had made a vow to God yet ran back to the sin that was so comfortable to me. But this time something in me had changed, and God wasn't allowing me to go backwards.

Forgiveness

"Instead, be kind to each other, tenderhearted, forgiving one another, just as God through Christ has forgiven you."
(Ephesians 4:32 NLT)

My senior season at Columbus State ended with me playing about sixty seconds in the first round of our conference tournament. I was once one of the top 150 players in the nation and on every team's scouting report in the southeast, now I was only getting garbage minutes. "Oh, how the mighty have fallen" is what I thought to myself as I sat on the bench and reflected on my journey up to that point. I couldn't believe I fell off like that. My Love for the game had dwindled. I once played with so much passion that my dad would have to tell me to calm down, but now that passion had faded, and I couldn't wait for it to be over.

We lost by a slim margin that night and I considered it to be my farewell to basketball. Sitting on the bench wasn't the way I envisioned going out; I was a fighter, but I could no longer fight for this game. And as I lied on my bed that night, I decided to let go of basketball; and a part of me was cool with that.

A couple weeks went by, and I hadn't touched a basketball. I was focusing my energy on letting go of the past and forgiving myself. I had been listening to Pastor Dollar and during one of his messages it dawned on me that I had been blaming everyone but myself for the position that I was in. I blamed Coach Preston for my shortcomings at Kennesaw, and Coach Moore for my shortcomings at Columbus. Then I began to blame the politics of the game for me not being as successful as I should have been. And yes, there were external factors that played a part, but ultimately, it was my fault. If I was ever going to truly move on, I would need to accept responsibility.

Nick and I were sitting on the couch one day when we got the news that Kennesaw had just fired Coach Preston. I sat there for a moment to process it. A part of me felt like that's what he deserved, but an even larger part of me felt so much compassion for him. I jumped up and went to grab my computer. I sent Coach Preston an email saying that I heard about what happened and even though he and I didn't always see eye to eye, I was praying for him and his family. Most people would probably say that I didn't have to do that, but I felt I did. I still had ill feelings toward him, and I had come to realize that those feelings acted as a weight that prevented me from moving forward. If I wanted to start progressing, I needed to forgive. As I formulated that email, it felt as though I was walking up to the mouth of a cave which inhabited a fire breathing dragon. This dragon couldn't be slayed by sword like in some mythical tale, but with humility. Sending it wasn't easy, but the things worth having in life never are; and freedom from my past was definitely worth it.

I never received a reply from that email, but the point of sending it wasn't to get something… It was to let go of something.

My dream of becoming a professional basketball player seemed out of reach. I hadn't consistently performed well enough to garner the attention of scouts. Agents weren't reaching out to represent me and try to put me in contact with overseas teams either. I felt like I had failed my mission. I felt like all the work I had put in since I was a child and everything I had gone through was in vain. At this point, I just wanted to graduate and get on with my life.

I started going to the rec center on campus and playing ball with some of my teammates throughout the week. I was reluctant at first, but basketball is therapeutic. There was nothing better than getting out of class and going to the gym to hoop; or in some of our cases, not going to class but instead going to the gym to hoop. We would play for hours. There were no referees, no coaches, and no politics; it was just pure basketball, the way God intended it to be. The game in that state was so beautiful to me. It brought me back to when I watched my dad play in that men's league all those years ago. For a long time, I hadn't enjoyed the game the way I once did but playing freely in the rec center changed that. I was starting to fall in Love with basketball again.

As summer approached, Nick told me about a camp that his uncle was hosting in Atlanta for players looking to go and play overseas. Nick's uncle was something like a sports agent. He had connections when it came to overseas basketball and had been helping players get to the professional leagues in different countries for more than a decade. For the last few years, to play professionally overseas was my goal. Making it to the NBA out of college was going to be a bit of a stretch for me; So, my plan was to play overseas for a while and hopefully have a shot at the NBA in a couple years. But with everything that I had gone through with coaches and the politics of basketball, I wasn't sure it was something that I wanted to participate in. I wasn't sure if professional basketball was for me, and I was afraid of not making it.

"It sounds cool, but I don't know if it's for me man" is what

I told Nick when he first brought the camp to my attention. Nick knew that basketball had left a bad taste in my mouth, and he knew that I would have some reservations about going. But Nick knew me, and he knew that I Loved the game too much to just walk away. So, him being the master negotiator that he is, struck a deal with me. "IF you go to this camp and you don't do well, I won't sweat you about playing anymore," he proposed. A part of me started to believe that maybe I just wasn't that good of a player. Maybe Coach Preston was right about me. Maybe I thought I was better than what I really was. Maybe my lack of playing time was completely warranted. But nothing brought me joy like basketball. The joy that it gave me was contagious. The game had given me the opportunity to travel and see things that most people didn't get a chance to. It instilled skills in me that I couldn't learn from a textbook. It also helped me form relationships that would last a lifetime. I owed it to the game to give it one last shot. "Alright, you've got a deal."

If I was going to do this, I needed to properly prepare myself. I had just over a month to get ready which was more than enough time. The only obstacle was that I was going to be doing this alone. Nick had graduated, and went to Atlanta to stay with his uncle, and Bejay had gone home for the summer. I still had two semesters left until I graduated and was in the middle of a summer class. I had grown accustomed to working out with other people. But now there was no one there to hold me accountable. No one there to stop me from taking shortcuts. In addition to taking a summer class, Chris hooked me up with a job working at a rec center with the city of Columbus. I believe there are moments and periods of our lives that help better define who we are; this was one of those periods for me.

I had a job, responsibility, and I was working towards something that I was passionate about. This was my first time being in a situation where I had all those things at the same time, and there was no one there to hold my hand. So, if it didn't work out, I'd have no one to blame but myself.

I had to be up by 5am to get to work at 6am. When I got off at 12pm, I would go to the rec center and workout; I'd spend about thirty minutes lifting weights, and forty-five minutes to an hour doing skill work on the court. Class was sprinkled in on certain afternoons throughout the week. This would be my schedule for the first month of summer.

A few weeks later it was time for camp, and honestly, I didn't know how I was going to fare; but I knew that I didn't cheat myself. I was up at 5am every day, and I was never late for work. Although my workouts weren't overly intense, I pushed myself every time I stepped in the gym. I also turned in every assignment for the class I was taking. I was consistent throughout that preparation period; and for the first time in a long time, I didn't take any shortcuts, even when things got difficult.

At this camp there were players that I had played against during my collegiate career. There were also players who had already played overseas and were looking to get back over there. Throughout the drills and the games, I stood out amongst the small forwards, and was probably the most versatile player in the showcase. Some of the players in the camp had won awards for their performances during their collegiate careers such as being named to all-conference teams. The only award I won during college was for academics during my first two years at Kennesaw. Throughout this camp I realized that the players who were held in higher regard than me in college weren't better than me at all. Lots of the issues I had on the court came because I began second guessing myself, but this showcase gave me the opportunity that I needed. It gave me the opportunity to play freely, and not worry about making mistakes.

Nick and I both finished among the top twenty players in the camp, therefore I had to uphold my end of the deal that I made with him. I had to keep going. A few months earlier I was ready to walk away from the game for good, but from the closing of my collegiate career to the summation of the showcase, I saw that I still had a lot of Love for the game of basketball; and I wasn't quite ready to let go.

The Return

"We can make our plans, but The Lord determines our steps."
(Proverbs 16:9 NLT)

After my showing at the camp in Atlanta, I wanted to go and play overseas as soon as I possibly could, and I started connecting with agents that could make that happen for me. All the doubts that I had about me not being good enough were gone. The camp helped me regain perhaps the most important ingredient of being an athlete, confidence. There was only one problem, I still had about a year of school left. Friends and family suggested that I could take classes either online or during the off season, but even though that was a sensible option, I wasn't sold on it. There are numerous places throughout The Bible that talk about seeking wise counsel. Proverbs 13:20 says, "Walk with the wise and become wise…" I had a mentor who coached on the collegiate level, and although everyone around me was saying that going to play overseas without finishing school was ok, he told me something completely contrary. "Finish school first, because once you get out there and you're playing and training, you're not going to want to go back to school. And then you'll never finish." Agents, general managers, and coaches saw breaks in your playing career as a red flag, and if I were to put my pursuit on hold until I graduated, it would show that I hadn't played for anyone in over a year; and I knew that would absolutely kill my chances of making it. But I knew that if I didn't finish, I would be one of those guys that allowed the game of basketball to use me instead of me using it like the tool it was. So, I listened to my mentor and decided it was best that I stayed in school.

I was telling my dad what my plan was, and he suggested that I come back to Kennesaw to finish up my degree program. I didn't like the idea of going back to a school that I had just transferred from a year prior. What will people say? What will the coaching staff and my former teammates say when they see me back on campus? But I missed Kennesaw, I missed Atlanta, and I missed my family. Columbus was cool, but it was a place of exile for me. Sometimes God will move you to a place or environment where you can hear him better. God had been trying to speak to me during my time at Kennesaw, but there were too many distractions around. So, He had to expel me to a place where I would be able to hear Him. I thought about those three Kennesaw State campus buses I saw on my way to Columbus and how I got the feeling that I wasn't finished with Kennesaw; that confounded me for quite some time, but now it started to make sense.

I reached out to the department chair of my sport management program at Kennesaw, Dr. Jim Calloway, to schedule a meeting about the number of credit hours I would need to graduate. Dr. Calloway was a cool individual, and my all-time favorite college professor. He helped organize the Olympics in Atlanta back in 1996. I thought that was one of the coolest things because I was at the Olympics in 1996, matter of fact, my family and I left Centennial Olympic Park moments before it was bombed.

I did my best to get in contact with Dr. Calloway. I sent emails, text messages, and called him numerous times, but I got no response. After about two weeks of reaching out I gave up. I was disappointed because I was looking forward to going back. I had been in Columbus for eleven months, which was the longest I had ever been away from home. I came to the conclusion that maybe this was God's plan, and this is where He wanted me to be.

One morning, as I was preparing to leave for class, I sat on the couch with my feet on the table eating a bowl of Raisin Bran. Kirk Franklin was playing from my iHome speaker when my phone rang. My phone was laying on my nightstand, and I had no intentions on getting up to answer it, but I felt compelled to go and pick it up. I jumped off the couch and walked to the phone only to see it was Dr. Calloway calling. Almost choking on a spoonful of Raisin Bran, I cut the music off and quickly answered.

"Hey Dr. Calloway!" I said as I harshly swallowed a cluster of raisins. "Hey Brandon! How are you?" Dr. Calloway and I caught up for a second and then I told him my plan. He scheduled a time for me to come and meet with him about a week or so later to discuss what I would need to graduate. I was happy that I had finally got in touch with Dr. Calloway, but I found it odd that when I stopped worrying about how I was going to get in contact with him and just let things flow, he reached out to me. I didn't know what to make of it, but I knew there was a spiritual aspect to it; and as time went on, I kept that event in my mind.

It was July 2014 when I went to meet with Dr. Calloway. It felt good being back on campus, not much had changed during my time away. I felt like I was back home. I felt like I was where I belonged. "Six classes and an internship are all you need; you can be done in a year!" Dr. Calloway said as I sat across from him in his corner office. If I were to stay in Columbus, I would have only needed five classes to finish; and I would have finished around the same time. But I didn't care about the amount of time it would take to finish. I wanted to be a Kennesaw State Alum, and I wanted that degree in Sport Management. I had put in so much work for it, it was only right that I finish the job. So, I made the decision to come back and finish my collegiate career as a Kennesaw State Owl.

There would be a few differences for me this go-round at Kennesaw though, the biggest being that I wasn't staying on campus. I was living at home in Tucker, which was about forty-five minutes away, and I'd be taking classes two days a week. To make it easy on me, one of my best friends Danielle Jackson allowed me to stay with her a couple days out of the week.

Danielle and I had known each other since high school. Matter of fact, our families were both from Decatur and had gone to school together as well. She transferred to Kennesaw before I left after, and she was one of the only people that I could trust. She also played basketball and ran track at Kennesaw. One of the things I admired about Danielle was that even though we had similar upbringings and were from the same place, she challenged me to look at things from other perspectives. She wasn't one of those people that just agreed with everything I said, she was quick to tell me "Nah, I don't agree with that." But for all the times our ideas differed, we also meshed extremely well. We were always able to bounce ideas off one another and keep each other motivated and uplifted. That's what real friends do in my opinion.

When I first came to Kennesaw in 2010, I entered with the wrong mindset. Now I was near the finish line, and I had to ensure that my priorities were in the right place. Basketball and school were my focus, which meant that I had to end things with Olivia. She didn't take it well and assumed that I was going to go back to being the old Brandon, the guy going to parties and running after women; But I was beyond that at this point. I knew her, and I knew the amount of attention that I was going to have to give to keep her happy, and if I was going to finish college within the year, I needed to channel that attention elsewhere.

One night she confronted me in the parking lot of Danielle's apartments. She had been calling me all day, and I was ignoring her calls. I didn't have much to say, and we had been talking about the same thing for over a week. She thought that I left her for Danielle which wasn't the case. She yelled, screamed, snatched my chain off my neck, and ran into my car before running through a stop sign and almost crashing into another driver. I stood there shocked at what just happened, but I understood it. I knew the pain that I put her through the past couple years, and her anger was completely warranted. I wasn't even mad at her, I just accepted responsibility. In that moment, I realized how important honesty was. I thought that if I would have just been honest with Olivia about things years ago, I wouldn't have put her through so much drama. I also decided that it was best for me not to date anyone for a while; I had to discover who Brandon Dawson was before attempting to share my world with anyone else.

While I was using this time to further explore my identity, Rahn hooked me up with a job at the law firm where he worked to keep a few bucks in my pocket while I finished school. I was hired as a mail/file clerk, and I worked there on the days I didn't have class. I learned a lot about life and the "real world" working there. I enjoyed my time there, as well as the people. But there was a common theme amongst the firm. I noticed that a lot of the people who worked there weren't happy and were looking for their way out. It wasn't that they disliked the firm, or the people, it was the everyday grind, and the long hours. Ultimately, they wanted their freedom. They wanted to spend their time doing what they wanted to do. They wanted to pursue the things they were passionate about and see where those roads led them. I related because I wanted the same thing. And although it was difficult having to wait to fully go after what I wanted in life, listening to my co-workers complain about their lives kept me motivated. I knew if I didn't go after what I wanted, that window of opportunity my dad often spoke of would be closing soon.

Opportunity

"Write the vision, and make it plain"
(Habakkuk 2:2 KJV)

During my final year of college, I played on a semi-pro basketball team in Atlanta called The Georgia Spartans. In this league I encountered a lot of guys who had already played or were still playing overseas and were in between contracts. There were even some former NBA players that came through and played a few games. I saw that I could play with those guys. But if I was going to play on the next level, I would have to overhaul my entire game. There wasn't one facet of my game that wouldn't need improvement, and although I knew I needed the improvement, I didn't know how to do it; I felt like I had hit a glass ceiling.

My coach invited me to this workout one night in Smyrna at this private athletic club. The gym was beautiful and reminded me of a Lifetime Fitness but smaller. We worked out for about an hour. He put me through all kinds of drills that worked on my ball handling, shooting, agility, and my explosion. As I sunk the last free throw of the workout, Coach comes up to me, looks me in the eyes and says, "Your game is here" lifting his hand to the bridge of his nose. "And if you really worked, your game could be here in just a few weeks!" Now elevating his hand above his head. He was suggesting that if I stayed consistent, I could break through that glass ceiling. After coach left, I sat on the baseline, slipped off my black and yellow Adidas Crazy 2's and reflected on what he had said to me. I didn't know if I was good enough, and I didn't know how I would get to the level that Coach envisioned my game on, but I knew I had to position myself for the opportunity. One of the main differences I saw between myself and the guys in that league was that they had opportunity, and I knew if I could just get an opportunity, anything was possible.

I graduated from Kennesaw State University on July 29th 2015. I was proud of myself for enduring and completing what I set out to do, but I wasn't fulfilled. I dreamt about this moment for a long time, but as I walked across the stage, shook the hand of the president of the university, and took my diploma, I still felt empty. Graduating was a huge accomplishment, but it didn't provide me with the satisfaction that I was looking for. I had always imagined myself having a big party when I finished college, like I did when I graduated high school. But that feeling of unsatisfaction didn't sit right with me, and I knew there was more to life than this. I knew there was basketball, and I was counting on it to give me the satisfaction and fulfillment I was so desperately seeking. So instead of having a party or a cookout, I found myself in the gym that night, doing everything I could to get better. My desire to find fulfillment wouldn't even allow me to celebrate one of the biggest moments of my life.

The following day I had a job interview lined up for a sales position with this company in Atlanta. I sat in the office and felt so out of place, but I wanted to give myself "options" just in case things didn't work out with basketball. The hiring manager was a big guy, he was about 6'4, 260lbs. We started talking about the aspects of the job, and afterwards he asked me if I played basketball. Then he told me that he used to play, "I was a beast too! Until I messed up my ankle", he said as nostalgia filled his eyes. Hearing the words, "I used to play" were weird to me and I never wanted those words to come out of my mouth. He then asked me, "Where do you see yourself in five years?" "What do you mean?" I replied. No one had ever asked me that before. "You know, like, where do you want to live, what kind of car do you want to drive?" I sat and thought for a second. "Well, I want to be a homeowner in Atlanta, I see myself driving a 74 Trans Am, and just living a solid and peaceful life." He looked at me as if he was in deep thought and said, "you know Brandon, I like you. I think you're a sharp guy. I think you can do this job. Another member of our management team is going to be here this afternoon. I would like for you to meet with them, can you do that?" "Uhhh, ya, I can make that happen."

I went to a nearby Subway to grab a bite and kill some time until I had to get back over to their office. While I ate, I asked myself if this was something that I really wanted to do. If I took that job, I felt like I would be turning my back on the game, but I didn't want to miss out on an opportunity either. Then I got a message from Danielle that read, "I had a dream that you were playing overseas last night. Keep going!" It felt like God was telling me to not give up on my dream. That was all the confirmation I needed, and it couldn't have come at a better time. I finished my sandwich, took off that stuffy tie, called back over to the office, and told them that I wouldn't be able to move forward with them.

For months I had been reaching out to agents and different teams trying to find my way into the professional basketball realm, but nothing had come to fruition yet. "I can tell that you have game, but I'm not sure if you have the stats that a lot of teams are looking for", was the message that I received from numerous agents. My dad and I made a deal that I had exactly one year from the day I graduated college (July 29th 2015) to live in my parents house rent free and pursue my dream of playing pro basketball. My dad played baseball at Alabama State University and had dreams of going pro before he blew out his shoulder. So, he understood what I was going through and that was his way of showing me that he supported what I was doing.

My uncle, Tommy Newson, was a pastor and had a church in East Point, GA. I was at his church one Sunday and he read a verse that hit me like the brick that Craig threw at Debo, "Write the vision, and make it plain" (Habakkuk 2:2). I knew then that I needed to put my vision for basketball on paper so that I could see it; and I knew if I could see it, it was tangible, and if it was tangible, I could have it. This was something that I had done years before when I was in a similar position pursuing a basketball scholarship. I pulled out a sheet of paper and began to write out my list to God. I made sure that I was specific and told Him exactly what I was looking for. I don't remember everything I put on the list, but I do remember the three main things:

1. Contracts for me and Nick Turner who was also looking to go back overseas and play
2. An agent that had a training facility and could get me in front of the decision makers for professional teams
3. A trainer who could help elevate my game

I didn't know how any of this stuff was going to happen, but

I just knew that it would. I felt crazy because some of the people closest to me didn't really understand the path I was on, what I was pursuing, or how I was pursuing it. But I didn't have time to make sure they understood the plan or all the intricate details, because the plan wasn't for them, it was for me, and all I could do was stay ready. I worked out in the morning before I went to the law firm, and in the evenings, I was in the gym working on my game. Up to that point, I don't think that I had ever been that motivated. I remember being in the gym some nights going through drills, and telling myself out loud, "I am a pro basketball player" over and over again. People passing through the gym probably thought I had some sort of mental issue, but I was keeping doubt from entering my mind. I had to tell myself I was a pro, even when I wasn't.

Through social media, I saw guys who I knew that I was better than get contracts to go play, and it frustrated me. I often asked myself and God, "when is it going to be my time?", which was the wrong question to ask. I was in a place where I was comparing myself and my situation to other people. I began to notice that as long as I was comparing myself to others, nothing was flowing in my life. How could I waste time comparing when I didn't know the struggles that person had to overcome to get where they are. More importantly, I began to realize that me comparing was basically telling God, "You haven't done enough for me, I want more", when in all actuality, He had already given me everything.

Comparing comes from a place of ungratefulness, and if I was going to get where I wanted to go, I needed to shift my mindset to a place of gratitude. Everything I did, I began to do it with a grateful spirit. Every push up, every sprint, every shot I shot, I did it from a place of thankfulness, realizing that even though I wasn't where I wanted to be, it was a blessing to be on this journey, no matter how difficult it seemed. I think the catalyst for the shift was me spending time with God in the mornings. I would go into the living room (you know, the room in your parents' or grandparents' house that no one is supposed to go in, even though it's called the living room) and read my grandmothers Bible. Grandma Pansy, my mom's mother, passed in February 2015 at the age of 91. One of the things my mom wanted was her Bible. She set it on the coffee table in the living room. This Bible was huge and had all sorts of family information in it; and as I would flip through the yellowish-brown pages, I would see scriptures my grandma underlined or put an asterisk next to. These were scriptures that spoke to her, one of which was Psalm 91.

"He that dwelleth in the secret place of The Most High shall abide under the shadow of The Almighty. I will say of The Lord, He is my refuge and my fortress: my God; in Him I will trust…"

Every morning that I stepped into that living room it felt as though I was stepping into God's secret place. I would always plan to spend about thirty minutes in there reading and praying, but thirty minutes would turn to forty-five minutes, and forty-five minutes would turn into an hour. I didn't mind losing track of time in there though. Often times this peace would envelop the room, and I would dread having to leave. Being in there became an addiction for me and was usually the first place I headed to when I stepped out of bed.

The gym where I trained was in Buckhead, right down the street from the law firm where I worked; it would usually take me no more than five minutes to get over there after I got off. One day I was going through some drills when I noticed two guys walk in.

One was about 5'10 while the other was closer to 6'6. They had a little girl with them. They started shooting at the opposite end of the court. As I continued to work out, I could feel them watching me. After about fifteen minutes, they make their way onto my side of the court. "Yo man, you go to Kennesaw State?" The shorter guy asked while pointing at my shirt. "I graduated from there a couple months ago" I replied. "You played ball there?" "Ya, from 2010 to 2013", I answered. "That means you played for Coach Ingle, I played for him too!" We talk for a while, then the bigger guy says, "we were watching you work out, you trying to go overseas?" "For sure, that's why I'm in here", I reply. He goes on to say that he knows an agent that's connected with the professional league in Canada and challenges me to a quick game. "If you're worthy, I'll contact him for you" he says as he smirks and checks the ball to me. I felt like Monica playing Quincy one on one at the end of Love and Basketball; except, I wasn't playing for anyone's heart, I was playing for the Love of the game, and my dream.

We played a quick game to seven, and I didn't cut him any slack; if he knew someone that was able to help me reach my goal, I couldn't afford to. I ended up winning 7-2, and afterward we exchanged contact information. He told me to send over some of my game films and highlights and he would reach out to the agent for me; I sent it to him the second I got to the car. On my way home I thought about everything that happened in the gym that night, and I was hopeful that this would be the opportunity that I had been looking for. But on this journey, I'd met so many people who said they would be able to get me here and get me there, yet none of it came to fruition. So, there was some doubt that anything would come from the exchange.

I got home around 8pm that night. I showered, grabbed something to eat, talked with my parents for a while, and went to my room. By that time, it was about 10:30pm, and just as my head hit the pillow, I got a text. "Hey Brandon, this is LT, I got your information from Al (the big guy from the gym). I'm impressed with your highlights." He went on to tell me that he was connected with some of the team owners in the Canadian league and minor leagues in the US. He also told me there was a combine coming up in Boston that weekend and if I was to sign with him, he could get me up there in front of the people who made decisions for these teams. It wasn't like I had any other options, so it was a no brainer for me; I met him at his office the next day, took the contract over to Rahn, and once he gave me the ok, I signed it and sent it back. Two days later I was on a flight to Boston.

When I got to the combine in Boston, there were players from all over the northeast; Myself and another guy were the only ones from the south. I felt as though I was all alone, but this wasn't a feeling that I ran from, it was one that I embraced. I'd felt that way my entire life. The closest I had ever felt to fitting in was with Nick and Drew and even with them, the fit still wasn't snug. That feeling of being alienated was comfortable to me, and even though I was hundreds of miles from the familiar, on the court I felt right at home. In a gym full of professionals and those aspiring to be, all eyes were on this kid from Tucker, Georgia. After the first scrimmage game, coaches and general managers were asking me what my plans were for that upcoming season. "Who do you have offers from?" "How much are you looking to make?" "Do you want to go overseas or stay domestic?" I didn't have answers to all those questions. I went from getting no attention, to now coaches, general managers, and professional teams trying to see what my next move was. It was somewhat overwhelming, but I welcomed it. This was what I had been working for.

About a week later, The Providence Skychiefs reached out to LT and said they wanted me. The Skychiefs were located in Providence, Rhode Island and played in the Premier Basketball League (PBL) which was an affiliate to the Canadian league; these two leagues often utilized the same players. They would sometimes send players from Canada to the PBL and vice versa. The Skychiefs invited me to training camp which was taking place about a week or so before Thanksgiving, so I had a couple weeks to prepare.

When I got to Providence, the only thing on my mind was earning a spot on that team. To some players I knew, trying to earn a spot on a minor league team in the US was a waste of time when the goal was to get overseas; but I understood the importance of not skipping steps. I understood that sometimes you had to do things that you didn't want to do in order to get where you wanted to go. I understood that this was just another building block, and the next leg of my journey. So, I went into training camp like a man on a mission. I ran every sprint at full speed, dunked every chance I got, and didn't complain not once. Camp lasted for five days and every night we practiced for three hours, sometimes longer. But I didn't care, I was willing to practice as long as they needed me to so I could achieve my goal. I didn't even give fatigue a chance to rear its ugly head. What I found out was that, remaining in a place of gratitude not only gave me mental and emotional strength, but physical strength as well. As a basketball player, I felt like I had found my way back to being the guy who didn't care about external circumstances, he just found a way to get it done. At this point in my life, there were no distractions, and nothing to hold me back. Everything and everyone in my life was propelling me forward.

When practice ended on the fifth day, Coach Kyle, who was the head coach called players into his office to inform them if they made the team or not. A lot of guys were nervous and stood anxiously in the gym as they waited for their name to be called. There was no doubt in my mind that I had made it though, and when Coach Kyle called me into his office, he let me know that I would be joining the Providence Skychiefs for the upcoming 2016 season. The following day I left for Atlanta knowing that I was one step closer to my goal. Even though I was now considered a professional in the basketball realm, there were still so many obstacles that I would have to overcome in order to get to the place that I wanted to be. As the airplane taxied down the runway, I reflected on how I got to that point. The funny part about all of this was that I almost didn't go to the gym that day after work when I met those two guys; but I kept getting the feeling that I needed to be there. I remember being tired of working out twice a day and wanting to just grab something to eat and go home. If I would have done that, I wouldn't be able to call myself a professional basketball player. I realized that your opportunity could show up on days when you don't feel like doing what you're supposed to do. But this journey is all about integrity and discipline, and you have to do what you're supposed to do, when you're supposed to do it. Or you risk missing your opportunity.

Preparing a Table

"Thou preparest a table before me in the presence of mine enemies: Thou annointest my head with oil; my cup runneth over."

(Psalms 23:5 KJV)

It was December 2015, and I had just signed my contract and sent it back to the Skychief front office. I was set to report on December 27th, two days after Christmas. I had just under a month to prepare and spend time with family. Christmas is my favorite time of the year and there's nothing I enjoy more than being able to spend time with my family during that season. I wasn't too enthused about having to leave two days after Christmas though, but that's the nature of the business; sometimes you have to do things that you don't want to do. But there was something happening that month that I was excited about; the release of Ashley's book, Surviving Your Own Jungle.

Ashley Dawson is my cousin and perhaps one of the strongest people that I know. Her mother (my aunt) passed when she was just eighteen years old and stepping into a pivotal point in her life, college. I was only eight at the time, so Ashley and I weren't particularly close, but I watched her from afar. I saw how she chose to grow from this tragic event and use it to inspire other people. It was always a dream of mine to write a book one day, matter of fact, I attempted to write this very book you're reading back when I was in college, but I didn't think anyone would read it, plus I hadn't lived enough yet. But now Ashley was doing it, so I was taking notes.

Funny story, like I said, Ashley and I weren't particularly close, well, not until it was time for me to graduate from high school. It was the night before graduation and most of my family from Augusta had come to Atlanta to celebrate with us. My grandpa gave us $100 to go to the movies; so, Nick, Josh, Ashley, my cousin Dria, and myself packed into Ashley's Toyota Camry to go to the theatre. Afterwards, we went to a certain establishment whose ice cream machines are always broken, but that night I was feeling lucky. We pull up in the drive-thru and order a bunch of food. I was in the driver's seat and Ashley was in the passenger, while everyone else was crammed in the back. As the cashier handed me the bags of food, I asked, "Oh, can I have a milkshake too?" I was then told by the cashier that the "ice cream machine was down." Me, being eighteen at the time and as foolish as I was, looked her in the eyes and said, "I should blow this place up" and sped off. We laughed about it all the way back to my parents' house, even though it was one of the dumbest things that I've ever said. It could have been considered a terroristic threat. But that moment brought us closer, and we began to see each other as brother and sister as opposed to cousins.

That year I spent the week before Christmas in Augusta hanging out with my family and helping Ashley prepare for her book signing. The signing was held at a coffee shop in downtown Augusta on a Sunday afternoon. I marveled in the atmosphere and observed as Ashley took pictures with people, signed books, and answered questions about her book and the book writing process. As we were packing up that evening, a woman came up to Ashley and started asking questions. They talked for about five minutes and then she left. When we got in the car to leave, I asked her, "who was that lady?" Her reply was so profound to me that I knew it had to be inspired by God. "When I first started teaching, that lady gave me a hard time. She was always saying negative things about me and just doing whatever she could do to tear me down. There was something about me that she just didn't like. She was downtown today, just walking around and she stumbled into the signing. She asked a few people who was this for and she was shocked when they told her it was for me. She felt ashamed because of the way she treated me when I first started teaching. God will always prepare a table before you in the presence of your enemies (Psalm 23:5)" In that moment, it became clear to me that we don't have to worry about fighting our battles or proving anything to anyone. We don't even have to worry about setting the table, all we have to do is take our seats. It's God who sets the table for us. He's also the one who goes before us to fight our battles.

That Christmas it was seventy-five degrees. We played basketball on the court at my grandparent's house in short sleeves. I even broke a sweat. I never imagined it being that hot on Christmas day. In my mind, the perfect Christmas would be cold, bone chilling cold; and there would be snow and hot chocolate. My brothers, my dad, Ashley, and myself continued to shoot around. I remember hitting five or six shots in a row from the left corner of the court, right where the cement met the grass. Each shot was executed with textbook technique. Josh looks at me and says, "you should be making all these shots, you a professional now!" He was right, I was a pro. I wasn't big on gifts because I know that's not what Christmas is about, but that title was one of the best gifts that I've ever received. That title came with something that I had been searching for all my life. That title came with respect. My idea of the perfect Christmas had been altered and this had far exceeded anything that I could ever imagine.

The day after Christmas, Dad, Josh and I went to Tucker High School to watch the Holiday tournament that was being played there. Tucker played first, and then we stuck around to watch another game. As I was walking around the track at the top of the gym, I ran into Coach Preston from Kennesaw State. I was somewhat shocked to see him there because he lived in Kennesaw, and Tucker was a good distance away; but then again, not so much because he Loved the game. We talked for a second and he asked, "What are you doing now?" I smiled and replied, "Well, I'm actually going to play with the Providence Skychiefs in the PBL. My flight leaves in about ten hours." Being the basketball fanatic he was, he was familiar with the league and congratulated me. He also encouraged me to try to get noticed by one of the NBA developmental league teams that were in the area. It was just like Ashley said, "God will prepare a table before you in the presence of your enemies." Even though I didn't consider Coach Preston an enemy, he represented a time of great struggle for me, and this was God's way of letting me know that He had my back, and I didn't have to struggle to prove my worth to anyone. If I stuck with Him, He would be sure to let everyone know just how valuable I was.

My flight landed in Providence, Rhode Island the next morning, and as I waited for team management to pick me up from the airport, it dawned on me that I was truly alone. There was no family, I didn't have any friends up there, nor did I have transportation of my own. It honestly felt as though it was me against the world. I thought that I had conquered my wilderness, but I soon realized that I was still in it, and I would have to make adjustments.

Before I left Atlanta, my barber, Eddie Gee, gave me some advice that still rings in my head to this day, "Don't depend on nobody for nothin." Eddie Gee had been cutting my hair since I was a little boy, and every time I'd go see him, I was able to receive much more than a haircut; he gave me wisdom. I told him about me going to play pro basketball and he told me not to depend on nobody for nothin' when I got up there. "If you gotta go to the store, walk or call an uber. If you gotta do laundry, find a laundromat. Just don't wait for people when you can do it yourself." Honestly, as I sat in that barber chair and listened to him, it was a turning point for me. I realized that my parents had been pushing me towards being able to fend for myself my entire life. If you really look at it, that should be the goal of every parent, to raise your child to not have to depend on another human being to live. Eddie Gee's words were the hammer that drove in the nail that my parents had started to guide since my birth.

For the first time I was in an environment where all I had to focus on was basketball. There was no schoolwork or any other type of responsibilities. All I had to do was workout and hoop; I couldn't ask for more. I would wake up in the morning, pray and read my Bible, then I'd head to the gym to work out and get some shots up. Then I'd go back to the house, grab something to eat and hang out for a few hours until I had to be back at the gym that evening for practice. I would often walk to and from the gym, which was about a mile away from our house; but on days when it was really cold that mile seemed like ten miles. I took Uber's when I first got there but one of my driver's was attempting to turn into a store and completely missed the driveway and ran us off the road, almost crashing into another vehicle. So, I figured it was safer if I just walked everywhere and only called the Uber's when I really needed them. It also saved me a good bit of money. I hated walking in the cold. The wind felt like it was cutting my face, and even though I had on my boots and thick socks, my feet would be frozen by the time I got to the gym. But Eddie Gee's words rang in my head with every step while I did my best not to slip and fall on the ice, "Don't depend on nobody for nothin."

A lot of my teammates would want to hang out and party. "Yo B, you wanna come out with us tonight?" They would often ask. "Nah I'm good man, Imma just chill," I would often reply. There were a couple times I went out with them, but at this point in my life, I wasn't looking to party. Even though I was a professional now, I was still looking to go higher. My goal was to get overseas, and I felt like going out to party and drink would only cause me to take steps backwards. A few of my teammates didn't understand that; they took it as me thinking I was better than them. This eventually created rifts between some of us on the court, and the closer we got to our first game, the more I could feel the rifts expand.

Ladarius Green, one of my college teammates my freshman year at Kennesaw, had also been recruited by the Skychiefs. He joined the team just a couple weeks before our first game, and it felt good to see a familiar face. But Ladarius was also another lowkey guy and wasn't interested in partying and hanging out, and this drove the growing narrative that us southern guys thought we were better than the guys from the north.

By the time our first game rolled around, tensions had grown even stronger. Ladarius and I could tell that we weren't particularly liked, but they couldn't deny our talent. We were both in the starting lineup and we each put up solid numbers, reaching double digit points and rebounds in our first game. This continued for the next few games until about the sixth game of the season where neither one of us barely got a chance to play. Some of our teammates who didn't have any hostility towards us asked us what was going on as we sat the bench for the duration of the game. We didn't have an answer for them until a couple days later when we both got the exact same message from one of the members from the team's front office. "There is a meeting at Benrus headquarters that requires your presence this evening at 7pm." Benrus was the name of a watch company owned by Giovanni Feroce, who was also the owner of the Skychiefs, and the jewelry company Alex and Ani. Feroce was also the youngest senator in Rhode Island state history. One Saturday Feroce pulled up to practice in his BMW i8. Every time I saw him, he was dressed extremely well. His clothing, although subtle, was expensive. This day was no different. As we stood at half court and listened to him speak, he used phrases like "sacrifice with us" and "be patient during this time." When practice was over that day, my teammates argued about what he meant. As I changed my shirt, I nonchalantly said, "they're about to stop paying us." "Nah, son, they gotta keep paying us", one of my teammates replied, but I knew something was up. I knew some changes had to be made. This happened weeks prior to Ladarius and I receiving those messages. Now, I had no idea what this meeting was about, but I knew that it was important because it interfered with practice time.

One of our assistant coaches came to pick us up at 6:30pm and we were at Benrus by 7pm. We left our backpacks with all of our basketball gear in the car while we went inside. We were met at the door by the team's operations manager and taken to a conference room upstairs. We had team meetings and events at Benrus before and the place was always buzzing. There were people, music, and food, but this evening the building was quiet. The only sounds that were heard were our footsteps as we made our way throughout the facility. We were led to an upstairs room, and as we sat and waited the operations manager dialed a number on the conference phone in the center of the table. The phone rang for about fifteen seconds, and then someone picked up. "Hello?" they answered. It was Coach Kyle, our head coach. Ladarius and I looked at each other and then we looked at the operations manager. He was directing us to speak. We looked at each other once more and replied "Hello." "Good evening gentleman, I'm sorry I couldn't be there to tell you this in person, but we as a team will no longer need your services." Both of us sat there in shock. They were releasing us. I had never been cut from a team, especially from a team where I was playing well. Coach Kyle went on to tell us that they had gotten plane tickets for us, and we'd be leaving within the next week.

 We went back to the car and our assistant coach that drove us there apologized to us, "I'm sorry it had to end like this, guys." I replied with my generic reply, "It's all good man." I have a habit of saying that even when it's not all good. I wasn't upset that I got cut, I knew that basketball was a business at that level, and being released was a part of the game. I was more so upset that they couldn't look me in my eyes and tell me like a man. It was like breaking up with someone over a text message. I thought it was a cowardly move. I would have respected them so much more if they would have been able to tell me straight up, instead of putting on this big production. But I wasn't surprised, I could tell that this wasn't a good fit for me. Overall, it just wasn't a good work environment. As we left the facility, I asked myself if I was still eating from the table that The Lord had prepared for me or if God had removed me from it. What I dreaded the most was the phone call that I would have to make to my parents. I knew that they would try to encourage and console me; and I appreciated them for doing that, but I was fine, and didn't need consoling. I just needed to find a way to get overseas.

The following day, we had to move out of the house that the team was renting for us. Not just Ladarius and I but all four of the players who were living there. There was another guy who the team was allowing to stay there because he was supposed to be some type of investor, but he was causing some problems in the house. On the night of the Superbowl a few of us were in the living room watching the game when we saw a few police officers pull up and run to the door. We opened the door and they asked if this guy lived there. We told them he was in the basement, and they came in with their guns drawn. A few minutes later they brought him out of the house in handcuffs. Apparently, he texted a friend of his saying that he was going to kill himself and sent him a picture of the gun. The owners of the house were notified, and they wanted us to leave. So, the remaining players were moved to another location while Ladarius and I were sent to stay in Giovanni Feroce's Newport mansion for the remaining time we had there.

The home was beautiful and located on the coast. It was also the highest point in Newport and had a view of Martha's Vineyard. I spent a lot of time on the flat roof, just looking out at the water and reflecting. Even though I had all this beauty around me, all I could think about was whether or not I was good enough. Being cut had me doubting my abilities, and if this was the right path for me. As I sat on the roof and looked out over the glistening waters, I wondered why this was happening to me. But often times when we go through situations, we don't realize that God is taking us through those trials for a reason. Sometimes it looks like He's punishing us, but in all actuality, He's saving us. A few months after I left, I found out from one of my former Skychief teammates that they hadn't gotten paid since I left, and that a lot of them were struggling up there.

I realized that if I hadn't gotten released, I would have been up there struggling as well. Getting cut from that team might have been a bit embarrassing, but it was a blessing in disguise.

Rhythm, Flow, Art

"So humble yourselves under the mighty power of God, and at the right time He will lift you up in honor"

(1 Peter 5:6 NLT)

The day after I returned home from Rhode Island, I was back in the gym. I knew that I had to get better, and I figured that getting back to my routine was the best way to go about that. I went through my warmup, then moved on to ball handling, and then shooting. But something felt off. Usually, I felt a spark when I worked out. I felt motivated like I was working towards something, but not this time. Now, I felt like what I was doing wasn't enough. I felt I needed more, and after about twenty minutes I walked off the court and sat on a bench on the sideline. As I sat there drenched in sweat from the humidity of the gym, I realized that I didn't know how to get better, I realized that I couldn't do this on my own. It was time to reach out and get some help. It was time to talk to Brent.

Brent Benson was a former professional player himself who played overseas in the United Kingdom in the British Basketball League (BBL). His aim was to now give back to those who were on a similar path; He did this in the form of training and LT had brought him on with the agency just before I departed for Rhode Island. I had spoken with Brent a time or two before I left, but my schedule didn't permit me to get in the gym and work with him. At least that's what I told myself. Despite the tribulations that I had gone through, there was still a thin layer of pride within me that wanted to show the world that I could do this on my own. I wanted to show them that I didn't need anyone to achieve my dreams, but pride had me blinded. I hadn't realized that there were people helping me all along. I think God sent me to Rhode Island to help me understand that if I was ever going to achieve anything, it wouldn't be in my own strength. It would be because of Him and through the people He had placed in my life. I texted Brent that afternoon with no greeting and getting straight to business, "Yo, when can we get in the gym?" He replied with an address and a time.

    The next day I showed up to Lifetime Fitness at 8:30am. I expected us to go through some shooting drills and maybe some ball handling and get out of there; And essentially, that's what we did. But it was on another level. Brent had me doing things that I had never done before like dribbling two balls at the same time between my legs, and behind my back. He had me doing full court shooting drills, and an array of other drills that I wasn't familiar with. If I would've had to grade my work out on a scale of one to ten, I would've given me a four (and that's being generous). That day, I learned that my game needed a lot of work, and that I was nowhere near as good as I thought I was. I realized that if I was truly going to be a pro, I needed to train like one. I could tell that Brent was only using that first workout to evaluate me, and that we hadn't yet gotten down to the nitty gritty. I knew that training with him would be tough, but I decided to give it my all and attack every workout. If I wanted to get better, this was the path that I had to travel, and there was no way around it.

    For the next few months Brent and I were in the gym three times a week like clockwork, and during this time, I learned what it meant to work hard. For so long I thought that I knew how to work, and I did to an extent, but now I was learning the benefits of consistency. Kobe Bryant said that he would wake up at 3am and train from 4am to 6am. Then he would go and relax and be back in the gym from 9am to 11am, then come back from 2pm to 4pm, and then finally from 7pm to 9pm. I knew that if I was going to get to where I wanted to go, I had to push myself in a manner similar to this. My schedule couldn't be exactly like Kobe's because our lives were different, so I had to tailor my training regimen to fit my lifestyle. I would wake up at 6am and spend time with God, run the trail at Stone Mountain at 7:30am, and then be at Lifetime Fitness at 9:30am, an hour before my workout with brent to lift weights before we even got on the court. Then we'd workout for an hour and I would be back in the gym that evening around 6pm. I had also started back working at the law firm a few days out of the week as well, so I had to schedule my workouts around that on certain days.

Brent was efficient, and his workouts were challenging. But no matter how tough the drills were, I kept showing up, and Brent kept finding ways to push the envelope. Whenever I thought I reached the extent of my abilities, he always showed me there was another level to go to. I had worked out with coaches and other players before, but this was my first time ever working with someone who trained players for a living. Subsequently, this was the hardest that I had ever worked. In the midst of my training, it dawned on me that working hard wasn't a skill that you were born with, but something that had to be cultivated within you. No one just decides they want to work hard, there has to be something that drives you to put yourself through physical and mental pain in order to achieve a goal. There has to be something that gets you out of bed every morning. There has to be some sort of motivating factor; and for me, that motivating factor was the fear of not achieving my goal. I had always accomplished my goals, but this one was more elusive than all the others. If I was going to achieve this one and keep my streak going, I couldn't afford to do anything halfway.

That summer, I spent more time with the game than I think I ever have; and I began to notice something about basketball that I had never picked up on before. Basketball was art. Every move, every cut, every shot, and every pass were like brush strokes on a canvas. But the game wasn't just a configuration of paints, there was a certain rhythm and flow to go along with it. It was like watching Tracy McGrady's reverse layup on Clifford Robinson during the 2003 NBA playoffs, or watching Kobe shoot that pirouette fade away jumper. Beautiful. It became clear to me that everyone had their own frequency with the game, and if you could tune in to that frequency, you could create imagery that could last forever. I was someone who appreciated art like Pablo Picasso's Blue Period or Hokusai's Thirty-six Views of Mount Fuji. I began to view the court as my canvas, and every time I stepped on it was an opportunity to create.

I was in and out of every gym, creating art all over Atlanta that summer. People who hadn't seen me play in a while noticed the growth in my game, but even though I was gaining the respect that I was once so hungry for, I still felt like a starving artist. The general managers and coaches of overseas teams still weren't ready to take shot on me. I felt like a beautiful painting that was stored away in a closet, instead of being placed on display for all to see. But I was no stranger to obscurity. I felt as though I had been under the radar my entire life. In times past, I craved the attention. I wanted everyone to know who I was. Back in high school, my goal was to be our top performer every night so they would mention my name in the sports column of the paper. Every time I saw my name in the paper, it gave me the satisfaction that I was looking for; but that wasn't true satisfaction, it was just feeding my pride, and pride is never satisfied. The Bible says, "So humble yourselves under the mighty power of God, and at the right time He will lift you up in honor" (1 Peter 5:6 NLT). It took me a while, but the trials I endured in college helped me realize that I didn't need to be the center of attention. If I just did what I was supposed to do and trusted God, He would lift me up at the right time.

Brent started inviting other pro players to our workouts. I was now working out with guys who played overseas and in the NBA. And to be honest, I didn't see what separated them from me. We all had strengths, and we all had weaknesses; and realizing that I was right there with them gave me hope. When you're trying to get into professional basketball, hope is one of the main ingredients. I was learning that sometimes you have to wait until it's your time, and without hope you'll burn out and give up.

One morning, Brent had to cancel our workout and I found myself in the gym alone. I decided since I was already there, I might as well use the time and put some work in by myself. I went through some of the drills that Brent would normally put me through: Ball handling, shooting off the dribble, floaters, etc. I was so focused that I didn't notice someone else had come in, an Asian guy who seemed to be in his early thirties. Between drills I looked up and saw him down on the other end of the court, just watching me.

After about 45 minutes, he comes down to the side of the court that I was on. "Yo, who do you play for?" He asked me. "Nobody right now. I'm trying to get overseas." I'd seen him in the gym talking to Brent before about certain guys who were playing overseas but I hadn't officially met him. "Look, don't stress it man. I've got guys playing overseas right now. You're gonna make it. You're a pro."

I'm a firm believer that sometimes God sends people to you to give you an encouraging word. The Bible says that death and life are in the power of the tongue (Proverbs 18:21). Our words have power, and I'm not sure he knew it, but he had just spoken life over me. I knew that I could make it overseas, but there was still that voice in my head asking, "what if you don't make it?" His words were timely and gave me the confirmation that I needed. He saw something in me that I was sometimes having a hard time seeing myself, which further solidified my hope.

Not long after that, Brent started working with Zach Graham. Zach was from Atlanta and played collegiately at Ole Miss. He and my older brother went to high school together at Peachtree Ridge. I'd heard about Zach but never seen him play. One day Brent gets Zach and I in the gym together. From the second I saw him, I could tell that he was different. I had been around pros before, but the way he carried himself differed from all the others. We stretched on the sidelines, and there was a calmness that seemed to be radiating from him; and as we went through drills, I could tell that this guy was the real deal. He had one of the smoothest jump shots I'd ever seen. But what really impressed me was his approach to the game. Every rep had to be perfect. He didn't look at it as just another workout, he took it seriously. He cherished those moments and understood that it was a privilege to play this game. He had a sleekness to his game that couldn't be taught, and for the next few weeks I studied him in and out. I paid attention to how he got his shot off, how he created space, and his decision making on the floor. I also noticed how humble he was. He had been playing professionally for a few years now, but he didn't act like he was better than anyone. He was approachable and held conversations with me all the way down to the high school and college kids that worked out with us.

One day, as we were walking out of the gym he asked me, "Where do you think you'll end up next season?" I pondered for a second, "I'm not sure man," I replied. "I just don't want to go back to the PBL." Zach laughed, and said, "Look man, you've done your part, and you've been putting in work all summer. Just trust that God will do His." That concept of trusting God has become so cliché in our culture. I've seen people say that they're trusting God, yet they continue to try and figure out how they can fix their own situation instead of allowing God to work; But Zach's words resonated deep within me. Pastor Dollar had been talking about learning to rest and trust God. He would often say that we needed to do what we had to do and allow God to do the rest. In other words, don't stress about it, trust that He will bring it to pass when it's time to bring it to pass. I felt as though God was using Zach and the Asian guy from the gym to give me confirmation that everything was going to work out as soon as I took my hands off the situation and fully trusted Him. I could see that God just wasn't training me for basketball but training me to trust Him.

Purpose

"But you are a chosen generation, a royal priesthood, a holy nation, His own special people, that you may proclaim praises of Him who called you out of darkness into His marvelous light."

(1 Peter 2:9 NKJV)

I never thought about purpose until I was twenty-four years old. My plan was to play basketball until I couldn't play anymore. But at some point, or another on the journey of trying to fulfill our own desires, we ask ourselves the same three questions:

What was I created to do? Why am I here? And what's my purpose?

I often thought about my encounter with John Paul Jackson. I thought about him telling me that God had frustrated my game and made things difficult for me when it came to basketball because He had other plans for me. I was now starting to see that God had done that, but I didn't understand why. Why would God disrupt something that I care about? I mean, don't my plans matter to Him? It's my life, I should have a choice in what I do, right? My Mom was still telling me that what God had for me went beyond basketball, but honestly, I didn't want to hear that. Basketball was what I had done for the majority of my life, and I couldn't imagine doing anything else. I had worked too hard and come too far to just end things here. I was too close to my goal.

I started dating this girl named Mya; she was from the Midwest.

"Mya from the Midwest" is what I called her. She came down to Atlanta after college. She was three years older than me, and we connected over our spirituality. God was the topic of a lot of our conversations. We talked about what the future looked like for each of us. She wanted to buy a house within the next couple years and continue to advance in her career. And me, well, I didn't know. The only thing that I was sure of was that I wanted to play basketball, I didn't know what life looked like outside of that. She was the first person I dated since Olivia, and I enjoyed the time that we spent together. But I also saw that we were at different points in our lives.

Mya was ready to be in a serious relationship, but I couldn't make that commitment because I was still finding myself. I still wasn't convinced that I had a true grasp of my identity, and I was too focused on the game. I didn't want to cause her any pain like I had done in previous relationships. So, we ended things, but as I look back, I don't think that we were meant to be in a relationship. I think God strategically placed her in my life to shift my mindset. God wanted me to get my mind on purpose.

Mya and I were going to a movie one night and when I got to her apartment, she had a gift for me. "Here I got this for you," she said as she handed me a book. I looked over the cover, "The Purpose Driven Life" by Rick Warren. I'd heard people mention this book in passing but I never looked into it. "Thank you!" I replied. I thought it was a sweet gesture. "No problem, I know that you've been thinking a lot about purpose lately and this book helped me a few years ago", she said. I was someone who enjoyed reading. I viewed reading as a way to escape reality. Oftentimes, the pages of books seemed to transport me to realms where I felt that I could be who I imagined myself to be. There were no masks in books, and I didn't have to put up any fronts. I could lower my defenses and I felt that I could finally be at rest. The Purpose Driven Life would have a similar effect; the only difference was this book would help to reveal the real me, while all the others only revealed who I once aimed to be.

The Purpose Driven Life was a 40-Day Devotional which covered five purposes:

1. You were planned for God's pleasure
2. You were formed for God's family
3. You were created to become like Christ
4. You were shaped for serving God
5. You were made for a mission

I spent time reading The Purpose Driven Life every day, and the more I read it, the closer I found myself getting to God. It became apparent to me that although our desires are important, nothing is more important than completing the mission that God put you on this Earth to accomplish. I began to focus more on The Lord and reach to the things that were important to Him, all the while slowly letting go of all the things that brought me no value.

July is a big month for basketball in Las Vegas. The NBA Summer League is out there amid other showcases for players trying to achieve their dreams of playing professionally overseas. I had previously gone to a camp in Indiana in April and was invited to another in Las Vegas in July. So, Brent and I trained vigorously for it. I knew that there would be scouts from different countries in Europe and other parts of the world, so I had to perform well. In a lot of ways, I felt that this was my last chance to prove myself and fulfill my dream of playing professional basketball.

I traveled out there alone, and the showcase was set for two days, with the possibility of it lasting a third. This wasn't my first time in Vegas, I had been out there for AAU games, a college tournament, and a showcase the summer before; so, I wasn't enamored by the bright lights on the Vegas strip. I had done that before. This was a business trip, and I couldn't afford to waste my time.

Like I've mentioned before, historically, I've always performed well in showcases, so I expected this time to be no different. I had overcome a lot and put too much work in for it to not. I thought that over the next two days, all that I've endured would finally pay off.

Even though I wanted things to go well for me at this showcase, something just felt off from the very beginning. The night before, when I was in the hotel getting everything ready, I went to pull out my Adidas Crazy 8's and noticed that they weren't in my bag. I must have left them in my car. The only other pair of shoes I had were my Adidas Crazy 2's. This pair was for casual use, but since that's all I had, I would have to hoop in them. I had only played in these shoes one other time, and the traction was horrible, but as I walked to the gym the next day with the Vegas sun beaming down on me, I thought it would be just another obstacle that I would have to overcome.

I sat in the bleachers lacing up my sneakers and scanning the gym. I saw players from all over the U.S. I also saw agents and scouts. I would usually feel some nerves as I stepped onto the court, but this time was different. I just knew that I was equipped for this. I had been preparing all spring and summer.

We start to stretch and go through some drills, and everyone is sizing each other up, trying to scope out who's going to be their biggest hindrance to gaining recognition from the crowd of scouts sitting in the bleachers. But as we went through those drills, I realized that my biggest hindrance wasn't going to be any of the other players. My biggest hindrance was going to be my sneakers. The Crazy 2's didn't have ANY traction and I had to constantly wipe the bottom of them. As a player, when you can't gain as much traction as you'd like, you become unsure of your movements on the floor, and it shows in your game.

We went through drills all morning, and in the afternoon they broke us up into teams so we could play. My team was set to play in the second game, and as I watched the game before us, I noticed the same style of play that's typically seen at events like this. Everyone was out for themselves. When you're playing in a situation like this, you kind of have to be out for yourself, but the key is to play the game the right way. That brings you more recognition than coming down and shooting bad shots time and time again. You can be offensive minded and aggressive, but you have to make the right play, when it's time to make the right play. Pass when you need to pass, shoot when it's your time to shoot. Never play outside of your skillset; only do the things that you're capable of doing. I had done a careful study of my game over the past few years and through my study and my training, I realized that basketball really is a simple game; players often complicate it because they're so focused on scoring. I saw that when I made the right plays, opportunities to score were inevitable. The same was true with life, if you made the right decisions at the right time, opportunities to elevate will be there. The key to all of it is being ready when the opportunity comes.

I often share with young players that you'll get chances to score in games, but will you have worked on your game enough to maximize that opportunity when it arrives?

The first game ended, and my team took the floor. My sneakers felt like dust magnets, and I could feel them collecting more and more dust with every step. I knew that I was going to have to rely on skill and putting myself in the right spots as opposed to my athleticism because of my traction issue. We transitioned up and down the floor a few times before I touched the ball. Normally, I didn't like to shoot the ball the first time it came to me. I liked to work myself into the flow of the game first, but this was one of the opportunities I spoke of earlier. A long rebound came to me in the corner, and I was in the right place at the right time. I take my time, fixing the ball so that my fingertips line up with the laces, elevate, shoot. All net. There's a certain confidence that comes with making your first shot. For me, it removed all the pressure, and it did the same thing that day. I continued to put myself in the right spot and make the right plays. My sneakers still had no traction, but before long, my focus shifted, and they weren't as big of an issue as they initially were. The game ended, and I sat down afterwards and untied my shoes, I was reminded of a quote that I once heard, "When you focus on your problems, you get more problems. When you focus on the possibilities, you have more opportunities."

The next day I planned to build on my success from day one, but I didn't have a good showing at all. I couldn't make a shot, I couldn't guard anyone, and made just about every bad decision that one could make on the basketball court. When day two was over, I left frustrated, and angry. I got back to my hotel room and threw my bag on the floor. I sat in the chair in the corner and held my head in disbelief trying to figure out where I went wrong. It wasn't the shoes, it wasn't the coaches, it wasn't my teammates. I figured it had to be me. Tears began to fall. I had been in some pretty low spots before, but I think that was the lowest. I was perplexed. I had consistently put the work in, and I didn't cut any corners. I couldn't understand why things didn't go my way, but you can do everything right and still come up short. This was my opportunity, and I blew it. I called my Dad, "What's up man, how's it going out there?" he asked. "I didn't play well today, Dad. I th - I think I'm done with basketball," I replied. "Now hold on just a sec, you're only saying that because you had a bad showing. It's ok, when you get back here, we'll figure it out. It's not the end of the world." He was right, it wasn't the end of the world, but it felt like the end of MY world.

For as long as I could remember, basketball and I have had this on and off relationship. When things were good, things were good, but when things were bad, they were bad. I felt like I had given the game so much of my life. I played through injuries, lost friends, shed blood, and at times put strains on various relationships all so I could play this game. But as I sat in that chair, I knew that I had enough. I was twenty-four years old, and I thought maybe it was time to walk away and start my life, a life away from basketball. So, I did perhaps the most profound thing that I've ever done in my life; I decided to trust God, and not just with my head, I trusted Him with my heart. I prayed a simple prayer, "Lord, look, I've had enough. I'm done. I don't know what it is, but whatever you want to do with my life, you can do it. I'll do whatever you want me to. I'm tired of fighting you on this."

Jesus said, "When you pray, don't babble on and on as the Gentiles do. They think their prayers are answered merely by repeating their words again and again. Don't be like them, for your Father knows exactly what you need even before you ask Him!" (Matthew 6:7-8 NLT). In my short time here on Earth, I've learned that God is big and complex, but He likes to keep things simple. We mess up because we overcomplicate things. In this portion of scripture, Jesus is telling the people, "When you pray, keep it simple, God already knows what you need before you ask." Have you ever been in conversation with someone who just keeps saying the same thing over and over again? It's pretty annoying, right? Well, it's the same way with God. When it comes to prayer, I've found that I've seen the most results when I've kept my prayers simple. God doesn't care if you don't pray some grandeur prayer, He wants your prayer to be real. He wants your prayer to be honest, and when I sat in that chair and prayed, He knew that I was being real with Him. I was at my wits end, and I was at a place where I had to depend on God; and ultimately, that's all He wants. We go through some of the trials we go through because He wants to get us to a place where we must depend fully on Him.

After I finished that prayer, I sat and thought about my current position in life. My goal was to become a professional basketball player, but what I didn't realize was that I had already become that. I played minor league professional basketball, and although it wasn't where I wanted to be, I had to be thankful for that because most players don't even make it that far. Just then, all the anger, fear, and frustration in that room was replaced by joy, peace, Love, and thankfulness. I was thankful that I was able to make it to the place where

I already was. I was thankful for the experiences, and even though parts of it were rough, I was thankful for the journey. The Bible says, "Godliness with contentment is great gain" (1 Timothy 6:6). I wasn't complacent, but I had to be content with where I was at this point, and the peace that I gained just from placing my heart in a position of thankfulness was unlike anything that I had ever experienced before. So much so that I called Nick Turner, who had been playing in Peru, and told him about how bad I played that second day; we had a good laugh about it.

The next morning, one of the coaches who was staying at the hotel told me they decided to hold the showcase for a third day and asked me if I was going. "I'm not going to be there today", I replied as I proceeded to get a waffle from the hotel breakfast. Instead of spending my last day sliding and searching for traction on a basketball court, I scheduled a visit to Count's Customs, which was a hot rod shop owned by Danny Koker in the Vegas area. I've Loved old school muscle cars since I was about nine years old; and I often watched his show, Counting Cars, on the History channel with my dad and I couldn't be in Vegas and not go visit his shop. Some people might think that I was missing an opportunity by not going to the last day of the camp, which I do understand. But there was another opportunity for me to take advantage of. By not going I was showing God that I trusted Him with my future, and if I was supposed to play overseas, He would make it happen for me. Basically, I saw an opportunity to trust God and I took it.

Completion

"And I am certain that God, who began the good work within you, will continue His work until it is finally finished on the day when Jesus Christ returns."

(Philippians 1:6 NLT)

When I returned to Georgia, I got right back to my training regimen and working out with Brent. I was also working with a few agents who had some connections to teams in Europe that seemed to be interested in me. I was hopeful and doing my best to stay ready. The summer was almost over, and it was getting close to the time when lots of professionals would begin to make their way back overseas for the upcoming season.

One night, as I was scrolling through social media, I saw that a few guys who I played against had signed with pro teams for the upcoming season and were preparing to leave. Before Vegas, I would have felt some type of way and wondered when I would get that call. Seeing that kind of stuff often made me feel like God had forgotten about me, but not this time. This time I was happy for those guys. I thought to myself, "they probably deserve it. I'm sure they've worked hard for it." Just then, Nick Turner sends me a text, "Yo, do you have any updated film of yourself from this summer?" I could feel the urgency in his message. I played in Brent's pro-am all summer and had some good footage from that along with some of our workouts. I was working on putting a reel together, but it wasn't ready yet. "I have something, but it's not finished", I replied. He responds in seconds, "it doesn't matter, just send me what you got along with your email address." So, I sent him what I had.

Two days later Nick texts me and says, "My team just sent you your plane ticket. Your flight leaves tomorrow. I've also added a list of things you should bring with you." Nick's team needed a versatile wing player. He showed their coach some of my film and I fit the vision of what they were looking for. I jumped off the couch and opened my email to find none other than the realization of my dreams sitting in my inbox. A layover in Miami followed by a six-hour flight to Lima, Peru was the final step in the manifestation of my dream. I stood there in disbelief questioning how this even came to be. I often thought about what this moment would look like for me. Would I cry tears of joy? Would I jump up and down rejoicing? Would I rent out a section at the club with some of my friends to celebrate? (Not my style, just threw that in there for kicks) But this moment was nothing like that, it was filled with gratitude and praise for God.

I'm not a fan of award shows but I always thought it was interesting that artists would get on stage and say that famous phrase at some point in their award speech, "I just want to thank God…" I often wondered if they said it because they meant it or were they doing it because it was the right thing to do, or maybe they had a mom like mine who told them when they were young, "if you ever win an award, you better thank God first!" But as I stared at that plane ticket, I felt like I understood why those artists did what they did. Throughout this process I had realized how tough of a task it is to achieve something that great. Maybe their journeys were similar to mine, filled with ups and downs and coming to their wits end to realize just how much they needed God to navigate everyday life, let alone achieve a lifelong dream. Maybe their gratitude was warranted, that was between them and God; But one thing was for sure, I knew exactly who empowered me to accomplish this, and to Him I was thankful.

    I'm a family guy, and nothing on this Earth brings me more joy than being around my family; I look forward to every gathering. I always feel at peace and rejuvenated when I get to spend time with the people who I care about the most. That weekend my family had plans of meeting in Augusta at my grandparents' house for family photos. The last time they took family photos was back in the 70's, and everyone had afros and looked like characters from Super Fly. But I would miss this gathering. As disappointed as I was that I wouldn't be there, I had to realize that when you're pursuing the things you're passionate about, you're going to miss some events and family gatherings. And that's ok, it's all a part of the game.

    I flew out of Hartsfield-Jackson Airport on July 29th, 2016. As I sat at the gate, waiting to board my plane, I realized it had been exactly 365 days since I graduated from Kennesaw State; and 365 days since my dad told me I had one year to live in my parents' house rent free while I pursued my dream. God is faithful and this was a testament to His goodness. But what I didn't understand was, why was He so good to me when I had constantly gone against Him in times past? I was a liar, a cheater, a manipulator, a womanizer, a coward, and had supported my ex-girlfriend in the decision to have an abortion; So why was He doing this for me when all these bad things were in my past? I pondered on that as the plane began to board, and I kept coming to one conclusion. God isn't good to us because we're good, He's good to us, because He's good.

Ultimately God just wants us to fully trust Him. A part of me believes that this dream could have come to fruition a lot sooner, but I couldn't fully surrender to Him until that day in Vegas when I allowed Him to take the wheel. That's one thing about God, He's a gentleman, and He won't take control until you give him permission to. When we give Him the permission, that's when we can rest, and He can work. But He can't work if we're getting in His way by trying to do His job; And for a long time, that was my problem. At the end of the day, the blessings that we experience come from our level of dependency on God.

My flight landed in Peru at 10:39pm that night. In my haste to get prepared for my trip, I realized that I hadn't done any research on the Peruvian culture, and my Spanish was no Bueno. Thankfully, there were signs in English throughout the airport that helped navigate me to my bags where I found Nick with one of the other players from the team waiting for me. Nick and I were happy to see each other, immediately jumping around acting like little kids. That was the scene every time we got together and is still the case today. As we drove through Lima, I relished in the fact that I was in another country living out my dream. It felt surreal to be there. We rode in an older pickup truck that had an exhaust leak that found it's way in the car, but I was so thankful for everything that was happening I didn't have time to care or complain. I just took in the view, and some exhaust fumes, as we traveled up the coast.

When people ask me about my time in Lima, I tell them it's just like any city that you would go to in America; You've got your good parts, and your bad parts. Our team, EOFAP, was sponsored by the Peruvian Air Force and we lived with an older couple right outside of the air force base. The part of Lima that we lived in was somewhat impoverished. It wasn't that clean, some of the buildings were run down, and there were dogs that just roamed the streets: In fact, there was a brown German Shepherd that we saw so often we named him "Streetz". But if you went just three minutes down the road, you'd be in what was considered the nicer part of town, Miraflores. On our off days we would go there and hang out at the mall and eat burgers and what not.

There was one other American on our team besides Nick and myself, Josh Chichester, who I previously played against in the PBL. Josh was cool, and the three of us not only meshed off the court, but on it as well. Many of the people could tell that we were American but sometimes we were asked if we were Brazilian or Dominican; But the people that knew we were American would often ask us questions like, "Why are black people treated so badly in your country?" None of us ever had an answer for that question. I was surprised to see that there was a large population of black people in Peru. Nick told me that there were slaves in Peru once upon a time, and these were the descendants of the enslaved Africans brought over by Spanish conquerors. It became apparent to me that there are certain things we might not ever learn unless we venture outside of what's familiar to us.

It took me a couple weeks to pick up the language but eventually I was able to walk into restaurants and order food and hold surface level conversations with people. I never believed it, but it's true what they say, the best way to learn a language or culture is to be dropped right in it. When it came to basketball, I didn't have a problem communicating. On the flight over, I wondered how I would be able to communicate with my teammates on the floor; the first day of practice, my teammates taught me how to say left (izquierda) and right (derecha), and that was all I needed to know as far as the verbal communication went. Everything else was based off body movement, eye contact, and hand gestures, which I categorized under the universal language of basketball.

It was surreal being in another country, speaking a foreign language, and playing a game that I cherished. I'm not one to shed tears, but I'll never forget being overcome with emotion before our first game. As I put on my uniform and stared at myself in the locker room mirror, my eyes filled up with tears. There had been so many highs and lows on this journey. There were so many obstacles and roadblocks, and I had taken too many detours. But every tribulation was worth seeing myself in that mirror. I could now truly call myself a professional. "Number 20", I said as I wiped the tears from my eyes. This was the same number I was given when I played for the Skychiefs. I knew that wasn't a coincidence; God was speaking to me through this number. A few years later I would find out that the number twenty was associated with prayer and expectancy. In The Bible there are twenty recorded dreams and twenty recorded visions. For twenty years Israel waited for deliverance through Samson. For twenty years King Solomon waited for the completion of the temple and his house, and for twenty years Jeremiah prophesied about the destruction of Jerusalem. Biblically speaking, it seems as though when someone is expecting God to do something big, He likens the number twenty to it. Which made sense because I was now twenty-four years old, and I had been dreaming of becoming a professional basketball player since I was four. That's right, I waited twenty years for this.

I played some of my best basketball in Peru, putting on display all the skills that I had acquired throughout my career. For the past few years, I played the game from a place of trying to prove other people wrong about me. I wanted to shame everyone who doubted me, but things were different now. I realized that if the greatest players to ever play were criticized and doubted, like Kobe and Jordan, what made me think that I wasn't subject to criticism as well. To take it a step further and apply it to everyday life, if people talked about Jesus, what made me think they won't talk about me? It was all a part of the game. I found a way to let go of the pride and ego, but keep the confidence; And now I played the game from a place of Love and thankfulness. I played it from a standpoint of expression as opposed to "I'm going to show you how wrong you were about me." In my opinion, the game wasn't meant for that. I started playing basketball because I Loved it and enjoyed it, and when I made my way back to that basic principle, the joy returned with it.

My best performance came when we were playing in the city of Arequipa, which was situated 7,661 feet above sea level. To give you an example of how high that really is, the "Mile-High City", Denver, CO, has an elevation of 5, 280 feet. So, Arequipa is 2,381 feet higher than Denver which made the air extremely thin. Two trips up and down the court were enough have you gasping for air. The air was so thin that oxygen tanks were placed on each team's bench. We had an older guy on our team who was in his late thirties and had been playing professionally for years, and during our three games in Arequipa, every time he came out, he needed the oxygen. Playing there was even challenging for someone who was as in shape as I was.

During the first quarter of our last game, I was really beginning to feel the effects of the thin air. I couldn't come out of the game because my team needed me, but it was difficult to maintain that pace. I didn't want to use the oxygen because I feared that would make me seem weak, and like I said coming out wasn't an option, so I did the only thing that made sense; I quoted scripture:

"But they that wait upon the Lord shall renew their strength;
they shall mount up with wings as eagles;
they shall run, and not be weary;
and they shall walk, and not faint."
(Isaiah 40:31 KJV)

And I continued to quote it for the duration of the game. Every time I felt the least bit winded, I would quote it. I must have said it thirty times during the course of the game, and what I noticed was that every time I spoke those words, I felt strengthened.

We ended up losing the game, but it became even more apparent to me that what I was meant to do on this Earth couldn't be accomplished in my own strength. The strength I needed, would have to come from God.

Love. Faith. Endurance.

"I know all the things you do. I have seen your Love, your faith, your service, and your patient endurance. And I can see your constant improvement in all these things."

(Revelation 2:19 NLT)

We usually had 1-2 off days a week, and normally we would go down to Miraflores to eat at Papacho's and hang out at the mall. But this day, we just decided to relax at the house. I stayed in my room and caught up on some of the Olympic track events. My room had an older television that was placed in a closet on a dresser. I didn't watch too much local tv in Peru, but every now and again I would turn it on and use it to help me pick up the language a bit better.

Lima was normally overcast and had temperatures between fifty and sixty degrees, but today it was warm, around seventy, and the sun was shining; It's light pierced through my window and illuminated the room. And as I sat in the chair at the foot of my bed watching the sprinters, God gave me something that He had never given me before, an ultimatum. "You can continue doing what you're doing and remain where you are, or you can follow Me and experience so much more," He said. It was the same voice that had spoken to me in the driveway when I was thirteen, and the same voice that told me I shouldn't be driving the night of my car accident just a few years before.

I knew exactly what His statement meant. For so long I thought becoming a pro would give me the fulfillment that I was so desperately seeking. I thought that I would be satisfied, and complete. Instead, I felt emptier than ever, and the hole in my soul was wide enough to drive a 59 Cadillac Coupe Deville through. God was telling me that if I continued to chase after basketball, nothing would change, and I would remain empty; But if I trusted and followed Him, He would fulfill me and give me everything that I was looking for and more.

If we're being honest, I had known for a while that basketball wasn't the final destination for me, but I couldn't imagine my life without it. I was too afraid to walk away. The game had been somewhat of a shelter from life's storms for me, but I had outgrown its covering; And it was now time for me to step out into the rain. I could no longer prolong the departure. Do you remember me asking you a question in the beginning of the book that I told you not to answer? It was along the lines of "what would you do if you had achieved your goal and now God was asking you to walk away from it?" Well, that was the question that I asked myself as the sun shone in my room. I could feel God waiting for me to respond to His ultimatum. I knew the ball would stop bouncing one day, but I always dreamed of a long successful pro career. Yet in the silence of that room, I realized that God's dreams and our dreams don't often align.

I thought back to my trip to Vegas a couple months before, and how I had told Him that whatever He wanted me to do I would do. I had made promises to God before. "Lord if you do this for me, I'll stop sleeping around" and "Lord, if you get me through this situation, I'll stop drinking", and the list goes on. I often went back on those promises, but this one I decided to honor. I told God that I wanted more, and that this would be my last season playing pro basketball. Immediately, the same peace that filled the room in Vegas, filled my room in Lima.

Within the next few games, I would see a decrease in my minutes that was inexplicable. I had just come off one of my best performances and now I was barely playing, but I was reminded of times past, and I finally picked up on the trend. When Bishop John Paul Jackson told me that "God had frustrated my game", this is what he meant. It was God causing me to not play at times in an attempt to get my attention. Well, He had finally gotten through to me, and I clearly saw that it was time to walk away.

We lost in the playoffs not too long afterwards and I returned to Atlanta on Friday September 16th. I was excited to be back home to see my family, this was the longest I had gone without seeing them. My brother, Nick, and his girlfriend, Kelli, picked me up from the airport that afternoon. When I walked in my parents' house, I was met by the smell of my Mom's world famous German Chocolate Cake. Basketball had taken me to another country and immersed me in a rich culture, and I truly enjoyed it; But there's no place like home.

The next morning, I woke up to a message from an agent. He was from Peru and worked closely with one of the teams that I had recently played against out there. The team wanted me to come back and join them for the next season which was starting in October. I sat there and analyzed the situation as I wiped the cole from my eyes. It was funny, I had worked so hard to get messages like this for the past year, and now they were coming with no effort at all. I thought about the promise I had made to God, and all the times I went back on my promises. But there was no going back on this one and I immediately declined the offer. I honestly felt as though God was testing me to see where my heart truly was. A few weeks after, I saw that a severe flood hit Lima around the same time that I would have been there if I would've accepted that offer. Homes and buildings were destroyed, and lives were lost. I couldn't help but think that if I wouldn't have been willing to honor God, I might not be writing this book if you know what I mean. For months after that, people would ask me when I was going back overseas, "I'm not. I'm retired", I would say. People looked at me like I was crazy after I would tell them that. The only person who understood my decision to not go back overseas was my mom. At this point, it was about doing what God wanted me to do, and anything that didn't line up with that, I couldn't afford to have in my life.

I would Love to say that everything fell right into place when I walked away from basketball, but the truth is, I struggled. For so long I thought I knew why I was created, and when I realized that basketball wasn't my purpose, it was hard to adjust. A few years ago, I took an enneagram test which is a personality assessment, but it's not just any personality assessment. Out of all the personality tests I've taken, this one was the most in tune. This test revealed to me that I was an enneagram type 3 which is labeled as "The Achiever." This meant that I was someone who was driven and success oriented, and that I was always looking forward to getting to the next level, which are good qualities to have; but it also meant that I was image conscious, and I didn't want to be viewed as being worthless. And since I didn't have anything to work towards at the time, I felt worthless. I didn't feel like I held any value, and that my best days were behind me.

Back in 2015, I received a message on Instagram from a girl who I knew from the track team at Kennesaw State. Her name was Nikki, and during my time at Kennesaw I would see her in the weight room in the mornings lifting with her team just before we started our workouts. "Hey, is there anything that I can pray about for you?" her message read. At first glance, I thought it was spam because I had never spoken to this woman, but I quickly recognized that it was really her reaching out to me. I wasn't the open book that I once was. My trials and past experiences made me skeptical of just about anyone who attempted to dig deeper than the surface of my life; but there was something different about this girl. Somehow, I knew she was genuine, and I knew she meant me no harm. So, I opened up to her. I told her about my grandmother being sick at the time and my struggles with basketball; And as I opened up to her, she opened up to me about some things that she was going through. Our conversation was so free and authentic, and it ended with us agreeing to pray for one another. We spoke sporadically throughout the year through text and social media, and before long, I began to notice how attractive she was; matter of fact, she was more than attractive, she was beautiful. We spoke more frequently in 2016 and we even went on a few dates before I left to go play in Peru.

Nikki was the polar opposite of a lot of the girls I had dated in the past. The music she liked, the way she dressed, and the way she thought was different. Usually "different" repels people, but her different was like a magnet that pulled me closer and closer to her. Perhaps the biggest difference was that she Loved God in a way that was unique for any twenty-two-year-old woman that I had ever met. Nikki and I started officially dating when I returned from Peru. She was with me when I was transitioning out of basketball and had a front row seat to my struggle of getting to the next stage of my life.

She was the most talented photographer that I had ever seen. She could make views that appeared so ordinary and bland, seem so vibrant. She had a talent for seeing the beauty in things that people often overlooked. Nikki had started this project where she would post a picture of something that she thought was beautiful every day. Seeing her process of finding the right angles of her subject and then editing the picture was amazing to me. Her passion was inspiring and pushed me to pursue something that had always piqued my interest, writing.

Writing always made me feel good about myself. Whether it was writing poetry or coming up with stories; Whenever I was able to put what was in my head on paper, I was at peace. At this point, I was confused and afraid about what was next for me. Often, I wanted to run back to what was comfortable. I started working in logistics, and absolutely hated it. I met some good people and learned a few things, but it wasn't me, and I dreaded going in there every day. One day when I had reached what I felt was my breaking point, I pulled out my phone, went to my notes and started writing. To my surprise, what I typed was a poem that was written out to The Lord:

Jesus,

I've been traveling this path for a while no,
 and it seems like an endless quest,
It's a cycle of trial and tribulation,
my patience is being put to the test.
I've come to the end of myself, realizing I don't know what's best,
I'm tired of carrying these burdens, so I come to You for my rest.

For a while I felt like I was on the bench-press trying to lift a weight that was too heavy for me, and it was now anchored on my chest. As the weight laid there, crushing me, I lost the ability to breathe, and was dying slowly. But after completing this poem, gratitude, and peace, along with air filled my lungs, giving me the necessary strength to hoist the weight off me. This was the first of many small victories that would soon follow.

I continued to write poems about the feelings that I had suppressed for so many years. I wrote about my struggles, I wrote about the things I overcame, but perhaps the most satisfying topic, was The Love of God and how it motivates us to keep moving forward in the face of difficult circumstances. Each poem brought me closer and closer to the completeness and satisfaction that I had sought for most of my life. Through those poems, God opened my eyes and allowed me to see life in a different light. I was once so unsure of my path, not knowing which way to go, and just following what I felt was right in my heart because so many others who came before me traveled the same routes. But those poems revealed my true path and confirmed that my path wasn't meant to be like anyone else's. I saw that we all have unique journeys set before us and it's our duty to embrace those distinctive paths instead of trying to make them resemble the journeys of those around us.

Nikki and I got married in October of 2017 after dating for less than a year. I had always told myself that I would never get married, but I guess I only said that because I hadn't met anyone who made me want to take that step until Nikki. A lot of people thought that we were too young, or we didn't know each other well enough. They said it was a risk, but I had grown to not be afraid of taking risks. I saw that great rewards often lay on the other side of risks. And as Common so famously said, "it don't take a whole day to recognize sunshine." I knew she was right for me, and it didn't take me long to realize it.

When we first started dating, I didn't want to say the wrong thing around Nikki because I knew she was a church girl and Loved God. And although I Loved God and was working on my relationship with Him, He was still working on me, and I had a lot of growing to do (I still have a lot of growing to do). During the stage where I was trying to get to know her and find out more about her background, I asked her about sex. "What do you think about pre-marital sex?" I was nervous as I waited on her reply thinking she would think all I wanted from her was that, but in typical Nikki fashion, she sent a reply that was so cool and smooth I couldn't do anything but respect it. "It's cool if that's what people do, but that's not what I do." My mind was absolutely blown. I had never been in a relationship where sex hadn't been the foundation, but it was confirmation that this was the girl for me.

I enjoyed being a husband, and it was cool to have someone to come home to and hang out with all the time; but I felt like there was something missing. I felt like there was something that I was still supposed to do with my life. I felt in the innermost part of me that there was something that I should be working towards, and then God reminded me of the poems that I had written while I was praying one morning. "What am I supposed to do with those, Lord?" I asked. Then I heard that voice, the one that had spoken to me in the driveway, in the car, and in Peru. "Put them in the book", He said.

At first, I didn't know how to do this, so I didn't. Instead, I did my own thing and started writing blog posts about God and spirituality, thinking that would suffice for what God had initially instructed me to do. This went on for a while, and the blogs did garner some attention, but it was exhausting to put those posts out every week. It became like a chore as opposed to something that I truly felt lead to do. That was probably because it wasn't what God had told me to do. When we do things that God didn't authorize us to do, all we do is waste energy and tire ourselves out; And He has no obligation to replenish our strength because we're doing something that He didn't authorize. One day as I was beginning to write, I had a mental block that wouldn't allow me to put anything on the page. Then I heard that voice again, the one from the driveway, the car, and Peru. "You're meant to write books, not blogs." I was afraid to write a book because I didn't think anyone would read it, nor did I think I was good enough to write a book. So, I downgraded my assignment and started writing blogs instead, which was ultimately disobedience to what God had instructed me to do. At times I don't know if we truly believe that we can do all things through Christ. Sometimes we like to put it on t-shirts and social media bios because it looks and sounds good, but most of the time we look at obstacles and get discouraged. That's because we're gauging them on our own strength instead of the strength that God has given us through Christ. I decided to take a break from the blogs and took some time to really focus on what God wanted me to do. I came up with the idea to use the poems to create a 40-Day devotional. The format would consist of a poem, a portion of scripture, followed by an explanation of that scripture on each page.

For about a year, I did my best to fine tune the book and iron out the details of the publishing process. There were some things that I didn't know how to do, nor did I know anyone who did them, but God is true to His word. Every step of the way He provided me with what and who I needed to complete this project. One of the people he put me in contact with was Millicent Bowman. She was a friend of the family on my dad's side and had a background in Education. Millicent was full of wisdom and energy. She was creative, but perhaps the most interesting thing about her wasn't her designs, yet the way she went about creating them. She never started a design without praying and getting direction from God first; Subsequently everything she put together was a masterpiece. Her life often seemed so "easy going." I'm not saying her life was easy because I'm sure she had struggles just like the rest of us, but her life didn't seem to be full of unnecessary obstacles. I think that's because the way she went about consulting God wasn't just limited to her creative process, but I think it was how she lived her life.

    I was so excited about releasing this book, I had always wanted to be an author, but there was only one small problem, what would people think of me? I mean, some people knew me as a basketball player, and some people knew me as a womanizer. Now I would be announcing to a large group of my peers that I was a Christian author. I often wondered what they would say, and if the stories of my past would come out in the midst of me doing what I felt I was called to do. I battled with those thoughts for a while, but that emptiness inside of me was louder than the potential thoughts of the people around me. I had to fill that void and moving forward with releasing the book was the only way I could see that happening. When I started to spread the word that I was releasing a book, I was surprised at the feedback. People seemed to support me and were excited to read the messages I had written to Jesus about some of my innermost feelings.

"Love. Faith. Endurance. Messages to Jesus" was released on April 23rd, 2019, and was met with support from people of all walks of life. The feedback was so heartwarming. For the next few months people communicated with me how timely this book was for them and how it helped them through situations that they were going through. Hearing that oftentimes made me just want to give copies away to those who I felt could be blessed by it. To be honest, I probably gave away more copies than I sold, but it wasn't about the money for me; it was about leading people to build a relationship with God. I wanted everyone to experience the peace that I had experienced, the peace that can only come from Him. Ultimately, this was about the impact.

That emptiness that I felt for so long was now gone. I felt complete, like I had finally done something that mattered. Throughout this process I realized that me outgrowing the shelter of basketball wasn't a bad thing; It was actually the best thing that could've happened to me. I saw that while I was under that shelter, God was preparing me through my trials and tribulations to step out into what I thought was the Storm of Life; but it wasn't a storm at all. It was actually an outpouring of God's goodness. This is what He meant when He told me, "Follow Me, and experience so much more." I was keeping myself from this "more" by trying to stay within the shelter of something that was familiar to me and was ultimately holding me back. I feel as though lots of people are in a similar position, holding on to things of the past when God is calling them to go to new places and accomplish new things for His Kingdom. For a long time, basketball had been my dream, but one of the most profound things I've heard in my lifetime is, "you can have more than one dream." When one dream ends, it's ok to dream again.

Basketball had been my dream for so long, but now I had a new dream. I saw how satisfying it was being able to help bring people to God. Hearing things like, "your book really helped me" and "your words were so timely" brought me more satisfaction than phrases that I'd heard my entire life like "good game." In 2021 I became a middle school teacher, and my students often ask me, "Mr. Dawson, why did you stop playing basketball to become a teacher?" I laugh whenever they ask me that because it's like they can't comprehend anything better than playing basketball for a living. But for me, the most important thing in life is being where God has destined me to be so I can have the impact that I'm supposed to have. Probably the most fulfilling thing I've done was help an elderly man who had read my book accept Jesus as his Lord and Savior just three days before he died. I think about that often, and how if I wasn't doing what God instructed me to do, that man might not have found salvation. Often times, someone's salvation or deliverance depends on our obedience to what God has instructed us to do.

Basketball was and still is a big part of my life. Some days I miss the game, and some days I'm thankful for all the lessons it taught me. Through basketball, God has shown me that true manhood isn't found in the number of women that you sleep with, but in how you stand up for Him. I saw that I was finally able to take off my mask because identity isn't found in what you do, who we truly are can only be revealed in Jesus. Through basketball, God gave me discipline, strengthened my faith, showed me how to endure, and displayed true Love.

If I could go back and change some of the things I went through, I wouldn't, because God met me exactly where I was during each trial. My only regret is that I wasted so much time by holding basketball in a higher regard than God. In the Old Testament, it often talks about how the people worshipped idols; and idol worship is simply the worship of someone or something other than God, as though it were God. They would worship things like statues made from silver and gold, and other items that they claimed to be God. Many people aren't doing that today, but lots of us have practiced modern day idolatry by putting something or someone in a spot in our lives that only God should hold. For me, that was basketball. For a long time, I thought the game could save me from all the adversity that I was facing; but on my journey I've realized that basketball was never meant to be my savior, the game doesn't possess that kind of power. Basketball was just my teacher; Jesus is my savior.

Family is Forver!

Atlanta Select days! My face might not show it, but I was so happy because my hands had finally gotten big/strong enough to palm a ball.

Tucker Days!

The bottom left picture is from when I was in the seventh grade and, the top and bottom right are both from my 10th grade year.

Signing day with my brothers!
From left: Josh, myself, Nick!

Josh's graduation from UGA!

All that fighting we did growing up really made us close

The Big 3!
From left; Nick, Drew, and myself

The night we beat Georgia Tech my freshman year!

Probably one of my favorite collegiate basketball pics.

Player introductions before a home game my sophomore year at Kennesaw.

My big sisters, from left: Tangie, myself, Tia. They eventually forgave me for the couch fiasco.

We took Nick to The Porsche Experience Center in Atlanta for his birthday party. From left; Chris, Nick, myself, Bejay.

Me and Danielle at Tia's birthday celebration back in college. I am not a Grizzlies fan.

The day I met Bishop John Paul Jackson.

Nick and I. From Kennesaw to Columbus, and beyond. Never missing a beat. Adidas, sign a brotha…

My cousin/sister Ashley's book release. This day inspired me greatly. Back row: Uncle Kenny, Uncle Eddie with his wife Aunt Florence standing in front of him, Uncle Dwayne, and myself. Middle row: Aunty Donna, Grandma, Dria, Grandpa. Front row: Jeremiah (JJ), Ashley.

One of the coolest experiences about playing for the Sky Chiefs was putting on a basketball camp for the kids in Cranston, Rhode Island. #BreezeLoveTheKids

First day of practice for the Sky Chiefs. Someone tell my man Deshaune no hand checking…

Me and Coach C at an Atlanta Braves game. This man took a chance on me back in the day when I was slow and out of shape and helped mold me into the player I became. Forever thankful.

Learned a lot from these two. From left: Myself, Rahn, Rob

Summer 2016. After Brent began training me, he started a pro-am league. Adidas, c'mon now…

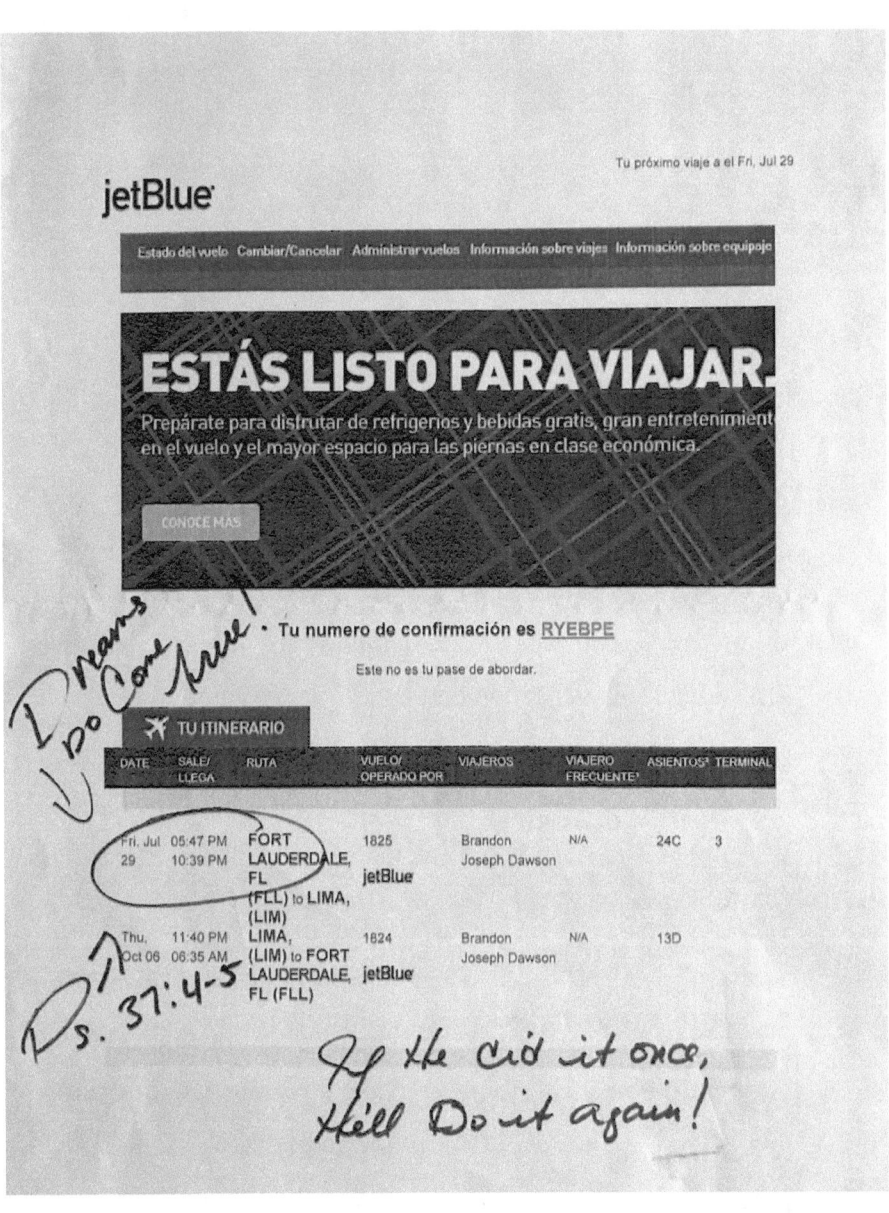

This is my plane ticket to Peru. When I realized it had been exactly 1 year since I graduated, I went back to Psalms 37:4-5, a verse I had been standing on for a while.

Out of all my basketball pics, this is definitely my favorite; because I envisioned this very moment, and it finally came to be.

After my first game in Peru this little girl and her mother approached me and wanted to take a picture. Couldn't say no to that face!
#BreezeLoveTheKids

"The 3 Americanos"
after we lost in the playoffs.
From left: Nick, Josh Chichester, myself.

Bet you didn't know Peru had their own version of "Christ the Redeemer" called "The Christ of the Pacific." Well, Nick did, and he drug me out to the most dangerous part of the city to see it.

We would go to this part of Lima on our off days and hang out. I forgot what these things were called but they had honey and cinnamon all over them. They definitely got my stamp of approval.

No real caption for this photo. I just thought my jump shot looked good and wanted to share.

My dad has always loved Porsches, so we took him to The Porsche Experience for his birthday in 2019.

No matter when or where we take a picture, Nikki is always going to jump on my left side. The bottom left picture is the day I got baptized.

Nikki and I with my parents (top) and her parents (bottom) on our wedding day. Notice how she's still on my left.

I Love finding old pictures of my parents; this is just a glimpse of how cool they are. Throughout the years, they've sacrificed so much for my brothers and I and for that I'm extremely thankful. Mom and Dad, I Love you.

Thank you so much for taking the time to read my story. I hope that it's blessed you in some way. If you wish to connect with me over social media, you can find me at the handles below:

Twitter: KingBreeze35
Instagram: KingBreeze35
Facebook: Brandon Dawson
YouTube: KingBreeze35

Love. Faith. Endurance.

www.ingramcontent.com/pod-product-compliance
Lightning Source LLC
Chambersburg PA
CBHW020136130526
44590CB00039B/194